SCTP: Stream Control Transmission Protocol in Real-Time Applications

James Relington

DEDICATION

To those who seek knowledge, inspiration, and new perspectives—
may this book be a companion on your journey, a spark for curiosity,
and a reminder that every page turned is a step toward discovery.

Foundations of Stream Control Transmission Protocol 7

Evolution of Transport Layer Protocols..10

Architectural Overview of SCTP 13

SCTP vs TCP and UDP in Real-Time Contexts....................................17

Multi-Streaming and Its Importance..20

Multi-Homing for Fault Tolerance 23

Four-Way Handshake: SCTP Association Setup 26

Chunk-Based Message Structure 30

Data Transfer Mechanisms in SCTP 33

Congestion Control Strategies 36

Flow Control and Buffer Management..40

SCTP Error Detection and Recovery...43

Path Management and Heartbeat Mechanisms 46

SCTP Socket API Programming 50

Using SCTP in Linux Environments 53

SCTP in Windows-Based Systems 56

Message-Oriented Transport for Real-Time Media 60

SCTP in Telecommunication Signaling..63

SCTP's Role in Diameter Protocols..67

Performance in Multimedia Streaming...70

SCTP and Real-Time VoIP Applications..73

Security Features in SCTP...77

Authentication and Integrity Protection 80

Protecting SCTP Against Flood Attacks 83

NAT Traversal and SCTP Adaptations 87

SCTP Over IPv6 Networks 90

SCTP in 5G and Beyond...94

Load Balancing with SCTP Multi-Homing..............................97

Reliability and Ordered Delivery Guarantees 100

SCTP Failover Mechanisms..104

Integration with WebRTC Components..................................107

SCTP in Real-Time Gaming Applications...............................111

High Availability Systems with SCTP 114

SCTP in SCADA and Industrial Systems................................117

Comparative Benchmarking with Other Protocols..............121

Tuning SCTP for Low Latency 124

Adaptive Streaming and SCTP..128

SCTP Simulation Tools and Testbeds 131

Wireshark and SCTP Packet Analysis 134

Debugging and Tracing SCTP Connections...........................138

SCTP in Mission-Critical Systems 141

Future Directions in SCTP Standardization 144

Challenges in SCTP Deployment..148

Application-Layer Protocol Integration..................................151

SCTP in Edge and Fog Computing 155

Case Studies in SCTP Deployment 158

Performance Metrics and Evaluation 162

Designing Robust Applications with SCTP.............................165

AKNOWLEDGEMENTS

I would like to express my deepest gratitude to everyone who contributed to the creation of this book. To my colleagues and mentors, your insights and expertise have been invaluable. A special thank you to my family and friends for their unwavering support and encouragement throughout this journey.

Foundations of Stream Control Transmission Protocol

The Stream Control Transmission Protocol (SCTP) emerged as a response to the growing demand for a more robust, reliable, and feature-rich transport layer protocol, particularly suited to real-time and signaling applications. Unlike its predecessors, TCP and UDP, SCTP was designed from the ground up to meet the needs of modern network communications, which increasingly require resilience, multi-path connectivity, and support for message-oriented data flows. Developed by the IETF Signaling Transport (SIGTRAN) working group and standardized in RFC 2960, later updated by RFC 4960, SCTP introduced a set of innovations that fundamentally redefined expectations at the transport layer.

At its core, SCTP is a message-oriented protocol, meaning it preserves message boundaries between the sender and receiver. This contrasts with TCP, which presents data as a continuous byte stream. In many real-time or signaling applications, such as those in telecommunications, preserving these boundaries is essential for maintaining semantic integrity and operational consistency. For example, in protocols like SS7 that were originally designed for circuit-switched networks, the preservation of distinct messages in transport is not merely convenient—it is necessary. SCTP allows applications to send and receive whole messages, thus removing the need for application-level message framing and reassembly.

One of the most significant advancements offered by SCTP is its support for multi-streaming within a single connection, or association. This concept enables multiple independent streams of data to coexist within the same SCTP connection, each capable of independent sequencing. In traditional TCP connections, all data is delivered in order, and a delay in one segment causes subsequent data to be held back—a phenomenon known as head-of-line blocking. With SCTP's multi-streaming capability, data in one stream does not interfere with the flow of data in another. This makes it especially suitable for applications that require parallel channels of communication, such as multimedia streaming, voice transmission, and control signaling.

Another foundational aspect of SCTP is its support for multi-homing. A single SCTP endpoint can be associated with multiple IP addresses, allowing for redundant paths between peers. This means that if one network path becomes unavailable, the SCTP association can seamlessly continue communication using another path without requiring reconnection or manual failover logic. This built-in redundancy significantly enhances the reliability and resilience of applications relying on constant connectivity, such as emergency communication systems, financial transaction services, or industrial control networks. In environments where network topology is dynamic or failure-prone, SCTP's ability to adapt in real-time without disrupting active sessions is a game-changer.

The association setup process in SCTP is another area where it departs from conventional TCP behavior. Rather than relying on a three-way handshake, SCTP uses a four-way handshake mechanism to establish associations, which provides better protection against SYN flooding attacks. During this process, state information is not stored until the handshake is confirmed, making SCTP less vulnerable to resource exhaustion from spoofed connection attempts. This adds a layer of security and robustness to the initial phase of communication, an area often targeted by malicious actors in distributed denial-of-service (DDoS) scenarios.

SCTP also introduces a flexible and extensible message format built around the concept of chunks. Each chunk carries a specific type of control or data message, allowing SCTP to support a wide variety of features without requiring extensive redesigns of the protocol itself. This modular design facilitates easy addition of new capabilities, such as authentication, partial reliability, and dynamic address reconfiguration. Because of this, SCTP has proven to be adaptable over time, capable of evolving in parallel with the growing complexity of real-time systems and applications.

Security was a design consideration from the beginning in SCTP. Unlike TCP, which was developed at a time when security threats were not as prominent, SCTP incorporates mechanisms for cookie-based validation of connection attempts, reducing the risk of blind attacks. It also supports the use of Authentication Chunks, which can leverage HMAC-based validation to ensure the integrity and authenticity of messages exchanged between endpoints. These features make SCTP a safer alternative in environments where trust and security are paramount, such as financial systems or control networks in utilities and infrastructure.

Another area where SCTP excels is in its approach to flow and congestion control. Borrowing successful elements from TCP while introducing its own enhancements, SCTP implements congestion control strategies that adapt dynamically to changing network conditions. Its flow control mechanisms prevent a sender from overwhelming a receiver, while congestion control algorithms ensure that the network is used efficiently and fairly. These mechanisms are crucial in real-time applications where timely delivery and fair bandwidth utilization can have a direct impact on user experience or system performance.

The reliability features of SCTP are also worth noting. Like TCP, SCTP ensures that data is delivered reliably and in order within each stream. However, SCTP also allows for partial reliability extensions, enabling applications to designate data as expendable if it cannot be delivered within a specific timeframe. This is particularly useful in real-time systems where late data is often useless and can be discarded rather than retransmitted, preserving bandwidth and reducing latency.

Despite its many strengths, SCTP has not seen as widespread adoption as TCP or UDP, largely due to the inertia of legacy systems and limited support in certain network environments. Nevertheless, it is increasingly being adopted in specialized contexts where its unique capabilities provide significant advantages. From its roots in telecommunication signaling to its emerging role in WebRTC and real-time multimedia, SCTP is carving out a niche as a protocol uniquely suited to the demands of contemporary network communication.

The foundational design of SCTP—combining message orientation, multi-streaming, multi-homing, built-in security, and flexible message structuring—makes it a powerful tool in the arsenal of protocol designers and application developers. Its ability to support robust, reliable, and adaptable communication channels is essential in a world where real-time data exchange is no longer a luxury but a necessity. Understanding these foundations is critical for leveraging SCTP effectively in modern, latency-sensitive, and high-availability applications.

Evolution of Transport Layer Protocols

The history of transport layer protocols is a reflection of the evolving demands and challenges of digital communication. From the earliest days of computer networking, when systems were isolated and operated on fixed schedules, to today's dynamic, global, always-connected environments, the need for reliable, flexible, and efficient data transmission has driven continuous innovation at the transport layer. The journey began with rudimentary mechanisms that offered little more than best-effort delivery and has since progressed to sophisticated protocols capable of handling the complex demands of real-time multimedia, high-availability services, and secure communications. Understanding the evolution of transport protocols sets the stage for appreciating the design and purpose of more recent developments such as the Stream Control Transmission Protocol.

In the early days of networking, protocols were designed with simplicity in mind. The User Datagram Protocol, or UDP, represents one of the first and most enduring transport protocols. It offers a minimalistic model, where data is sent as individual packets without any guarantee of delivery, order, or integrity. UDP remains relevant because of its low overhead and suitability for applications where speed matters more than reliability, such as DNS queries or real-time video and audio transmissions that can tolerate occasional packet loss. However, the simplicity of UDP comes with significant trade-offs. Without built-in mechanisms for congestion control or retransmission, UDP places the burden of reliability entirely on the application layer, which may or may not be equipped to handle such responsibilities.

To address these limitations, the Transmission Control Protocol, or TCP, was introduced. TCP fundamentally transformed the landscape of digital communication by introducing reliable, connection-oriented transmission. With its three-way handshake, sequence numbering, acknowledgment system, flow control, and congestion management, TCP quickly became the dominant transport layer protocol in the internet stack. Its ability to guarantee the in-order and complete delivery of data made it the protocol of choice for applications such as email, file transfer, and web browsing. However, TCP was built at a time when networks were relatively static and predictable. As such, its design assumes certain behaviors that can become problematic in modern high-speed or wireless environments. For example, TCP's congestion control mechanisms can sometimes misinterpret packet loss caused by radio interference as a sign of congestion, leading to unnecessary throttling of transmission rates.

As the internet expanded and diversified, new use cases began to emerge that tested the limits of traditional transport protocols. Real-time applications, such as Voice over IP, online gaming, and video conferencing, posed a particular challenge. These applications prioritize timeliness over reliability; a delayed packet is often more harmful than a lost one. TCP's insistence on ordered delivery can result in head-of-line blocking, where the arrival of one delayed packet stalls the delivery of all subsequent packets. This behavior can cause significant degradation in the quality of real-time communications. UDP, while free of this limitation, offers no reliability whatsoever, forcing developers to reinvent reliability mechanisms or live with an unacceptable level of data loss. This growing divide between what existing protocols could offer and what applications required created a pressing need for a new kind of transport protocol.

In response to these emerging needs, the Stream Control Transmission Protocol was developed. SCTP was designed to combine the best aspects of TCP and UDP while introducing new features that directly addressed the shortcomings of both. But before diving into its specifics, it's essential to consider other contemporary efforts that attempted to evolve transport protocol design. The Datagram Congestion Control Protocol, or DCCP, is one such example. DCCP sought to provide congestion control without reliable delivery, targeting applications that required flow regulation without the cost of retransmission. While conceptually sound, DCCP suffered from limited adoption, in part due to lack of support in existing infrastructure and insufficient differentiation from alternatives.

Another noteworthy development was the introduction of QUIC by Google. Built on top of UDP and incorporating many features traditionally associated with TCP, such as stream multiplexing and encryption, QUIC aimed to modernize the transport layer for the web. QUIC's integration with TLS for encryption and its focus on reducing latency during connection establishment made it particularly attractive for web services. Over time, QUIC gained traction and was eventually adopted by the IETF as a standardized protocol, becoming a central component of HTTP/3. This shift signaled a broader recognition that the classical transport model, dominated by TCP and UDP, was no longer sufficient on its own to meet the needs of modern applications.

Throughout this period of evolution, transport protocols have been shaped by the interplay between application requirements, network characteristics, and technological advancements. High-speed broadband, mobile networks, and satellite communications each introduce different challenges, from high latency to packet loss and jitter. Transport protocols must adapt to these conditions, balancing efficiency with fairness, and responsiveness with robustness. As a result, new protocols often borrow from the lessons of their predecessors while innovating in key areas. For example, SCTP inherited the concept of reliable delivery and congestion control from TCP but introduced multi-streaming to avoid head-of-line blocking. It also added multi-homing to support path redundancy and failover, features absent in both TCP and UDP.

The evolution of transport protocols is not only technical but also political and economic. Adoption of new protocols often depends on the willingness of infrastructure providers, operating system vendors, and application developers to support them. Middleboxes, such as firewalls and NAT devices, can interfere with the deployment of new protocols, especially those that do not conform to expected behaviors or port usage. This has historically slowed the adoption of innovations like SCTP and DCCP, despite their technical merits. The inertia of the installed base is a formidable barrier, and even protocols that solve long-standing problems can struggle to gain traction in a landscape dominated by legacy systems.

Yet despite these challenges, the drive for better transport protocols continues. As new applications emerge and user expectations rise, especially in areas like virtual reality, autonomous vehicles, and the Internet of Things, the need for transport protocols that can handle high volumes of time-sensitive data becomes even more critical. These use cases demand low latency, high reliability, and adaptability to changing network conditions, often simultaneously. The evolution of the transport layer is far from over; it is a dynamic process shaped by innovation, necessity, and experimentation. SCTP stands as a key milestone in this journey, embodying the principles of robustness, flexibility, and efficiency that define the modern era of digital communication.

Architectural Overview of SCTP

The architecture of the Stream Control Transmission Protocol (SCTP) is a thoughtfully designed framework that combines elements of proven transport protocols with innovative features tailored for the demands of modern network applications. Unlike traditional protocols such as TCP and UDP, SCTP introduces a layered and modular architecture that not only addresses the limitations of its predecessors but also opens the door for advanced functionality in real-time and mission-critical systems. At its heart, SCTP is a message-oriented, connection-oriented protocol built for reliability, security, and efficiency. Its architectural principles are deeply embedded in the structure of its packet format, connection management, and handling of data flows across diverse network paths.

SCTP operates at the transport layer of the OSI model, the same layer as TCP and UDP, and provides communication services directly to the application layer. However, its internal structure diverges significantly. An SCTP connection, referred to as an association, is established between two endpoints, each of which may have multiple IP addresses. This capability, known as multi-homing, allows SCTP to maintain redundancy and fault tolerance within the transport layer itself. Each endpoint maintains a primary path for sending data but monitors alternate paths that can be used if the primary path fails. This seamless path switching is transparent to the application and provides a level of robustness that is critical in systems where uptime and continuity are non-negotiable.

One of the most defining features of SCTP's architecture is its chunk-based message structure. Every SCTP packet is composed of one or more chunks, each serving a specific purpose. The protocol mandates the presence of a common header at the beginning of every packet, which contains key information such as source and destination ports, verification tag, and checksum. Following the common header, each chunk contains its own header and payload. There are several types of chunks, including those for initiating and terminating associations, acknowledging received data, and transporting user messages. This modular approach enables the protocol to be both extensible and efficient. New features can be introduced through the definition of additional chunk types without disrupting the core structure of the protocol.

SCTP also differs from TCP in how it manages data flow. Whereas TCP treats data as a continuous stream of bytes, SCTP maintains message boundaries. This means that each user message sent is preserved in its entirety upon delivery. For applications that rely on distinct units of data, such as signaling systems or transaction protocols, this architectural choice eliminates the need for reassembly logic at the application level. It simplifies programming and ensures that messages are delivered exactly as intended, without fragmentation or coalescence that could alter their semantic meaning.

In managing associations, SCTP uses a four-way handshake process that enhances the protocol's resilience against spoofing and denial-of-service attacks. When an association is initiated, the initiating endpoint sends an INIT chunk, and the receiving endpoint responds with an INIT-ACK chunk containing a cookie. The initiator must return this cookie in a COOKIE-ECHO chunk, which the responder then verifies before finalizing the association with a COOKIE-ACK. This mechanism ensures that no state is committed on the server until the client has proven its identity, significantly reducing the risk of resource exhaustion from malicious actors.

The protocol's architecture also includes robust mechanisms for error detection and correction. SCTP uses a 32-bit CRC checksum to verify the integrity of each packet, offering better error detection than the 16-bit checksum used by TCP. It also employs sequence numbers, known as Transmission Sequence Numbers (TSNs), to keep track of the order of data chunks. This enables reliable delivery and detection of lost or duplicate messages. The protocol can selectively acknowledge received data chunks using SACK chunks, allowing for more efficient retransmission strategies and avoiding the need to resend data unnecessarily.

A particularly powerful aspect of SCTP's architecture is its support for multi-streaming. Within a single SCTP association, multiple logical streams can be established. Each stream operates independently with its own sequence numbers, ensuring that delivery delays or losses in one stream do not affect others. This architecture solves the problem of head-of-line blocking inherent in TCP, where one delayed packet can hold up all subsequent data. For applications that transmit multiple types of data—such as control commands, media content, and telemetry—this separation of streams is invaluable. It increases throughput, reduces latency, and enhances the overall quality of service.

Flow control in SCTP is handled on a per-association basis, rather than per-stream. Each endpoint advertises a receive window indicating the amount of data it is willing to accept. The sender respects this window when transmitting data to avoid overwhelming the receiver. Meanwhile, congestion control algorithms, adapted from TCP but enhanced for multi-homed environments, manage the rate at which data is injected into the network. These mechanisms ensure that SCTP remains fair in shared network environments while making full use of available capacity.

Security and authentication are integral components of the SCTP architecture. The protocol includes support for message authentication through the use of HMAC-based techniques. This ensures that data has not been tampered with and that it originates from a verified source. Additionally, because the verification tag in the common header changes with each association, it is more difficult for an attacker to inject malicious packets into an ongoing session. This tag, in combination with the cookie mechanism during handshake, provides a strong defense against common transport-layer attacks.

The flexibility and modularity of SCTP are further highlighted by its support for partial reliability extensions and dynamic address reconfiguration. Partial reliability allows applications to specify expiration conditions for certain data, enabling more efficient communication in scenarios where delayed information loses its value. Dynamic address reconfiguration, on the other hand, permits changes to the set of IP addresses used by an association during its lifetime. This is particularly useful in mobile environments where endpoints may move between networks.

SCTP's architecture, while more complex than that of TCP or UDP, reflects a deliberate effort to address the growing needs of networked systems. It combines robustness, flexibility, and efficiency in a way that positions it as a strong candidate for a wide range of applications, particularly those requiring high reliability, low latency, and multi-path resilience. The integration of features like multi-streaming, multi-homing, modular chunk structure, and built-in security mechanisms within a unified framework demonstrates a thoughtful approach to protocol design, anticipating challenges that modern and future networks are bound to encounter.

SCTP vs TCP and UDP in Real-Time Contexts

The effectiveness of a transport protocol in real-time communication scenarios depends heavily on its ability to balance reliability, latency, throughput, and resilience. As modern applications increasingly rely on immediate data exchange for voice, video, control systems, and interactive services, the choice of transport protocol becomes a foundational element of system design. Stream Control Transmission Protocol (SCTP), Transmission Control Protocol (TCP), and User Datagram Protocol (UDP) each present different models of communication, with strengths and limitations that become especially apparent when applied to real-time contexts. While TCP and UDP have been foundational to the evolution of network communication, SCTP introduces advanced features designed specifically to address the performance and architectural gaps found in its predecessors, particularly under the constraints and demands of real-time operations.

UDP is the simplest of the three, offering a connectionless, stateless, and lightweight transport service. It is often favored in real-time applications like voice over IP (VoIP), live streaming, and gaming, where the timeliness of delivery is more critical than perfect accuracy. UDP does not ensure packet delivery, ordering, or duplication protection, and it lacks any congestion or flow control. This absence of overhead makes it extremely fast and ideal for situations where latency must be minimized, and occasional data loss is acceptable or recoverable by application logic. For instance, a few dropped audio packets in a voice conversation may not even be noticed by the user. However, this very same minimalism becomes a liability in scenarios requiring dependable delivery or robustness against network issues. Since UDP has no built-in mechanisms for retransmission or path failover, applications must shoulder all the complexity of ensuring reliability and recovery, which can lead to redundancy, inefficiency, and inconsistency in implementation.

TCP, in contrast, provides a reliable, connection-oriented transport layer with in-order delivery, retransmissions, congestion control, and flow regulation. It is designed for applications like file transfers, emails,

17

and web browsing, where accuracy and complete delivery are more important than speed. TCP's reliability mechanisms, such as the sliding window and acknowledgment systems, ensure that data is delivered correctly and in the intended sequence. However, these features introduce latency, which is undesirable in real-time applications. The problem becomes more acute in scenarios involving packet loss or out-of-order delivery, as TCP will delay the flow of subsequent data until the missing packets are recovered, causing head-of-line blocking. In real-time contexts, this behavior can lead to noticeable lags, degraded audio or video quality, or a poor user experience during interactive sessions. Moreover, TCP's inability to leverage multiple network paths simultaneously and its lack of support for stream independence limit its utility in modern, dynamic networking environments.

SCTP was created as a hybrid approach, incorporating the benefits of both TCP and UDP while introducing novel mechanisms aimed at real-time performance, multi-path communication, and robust error handling. One of its most impactful features is multi-streaming. Within a single SCTP association, multiple streams can transmit data independently. This structure eliminates the head-of-line blocking seen in TCP, as a delay or loss in one stream does not affect the others. In real-time systems where different types of data flow concurrently—such as control commands, audio, and sensor updates—this separation is critical. It allows the most time-sensitive information to reach its destination promptly, even if other less-critical streams experience network issues.

SCTP also supports multi-homing, enabling endpoints to be identified by multiple IP addresses. This provides automatic failover if one network path becomes unavailable, improving reliability and resilience. In contrast, TCP and UDP typically bind to a single network path, making them vulnerable to route failures unless higher-layer redundancy mechanisms are implemented. Real-time systems, especially those operating in mobile or fluctuating environments such as vehicular networks or mission-critical infrastructure, benefit immensely from SCTP's ability to recover without breaking the connection or requiring renegotiation at the application level.

Another distinguishing factor is SCTP's message-oriented architecture. Unlike TCP, which handles data as a continuous byte stream, SCTP treats each piece of data as a discrete message. This preserves application-level message boundaries, simplifying development and reducing the likelihood of errors during reassembly. In real-time systems where each message may represent a unique command or event, maintaining this structure is vital. The need to define and maintain message boundaries in TCP-based systems often introduces additional application-layer complexity and processing overhead.

SCTP's congestion control and flow regulation mechanisms are similar in purpose to those found in TCP but are designed to operate more efficiently in environments with multiple paths and variable network conditions. It uses Selective Acknowledgment (SACK) to identify and retransmit only the missing data, improving performance when packet loss occurs. Additionally, SCTP provides more accurate feedback about the state of the transmission path, which can be used to dynamically adjust the sending rate and avoid congestion-induced delay—an advantage in maintaining the low-latency requirements of real-time applications.

Security is another area where SCTP advances beyond the baseline offerings of TCP and UDP. SCTP's built-in cookie mechanism during the four-way handshake process guards against SYN flood attacks and spoofed connections more effectively than TCP's three-way handshake. Furthermore, the optional support for message authentication through HMAC ensures that data integrity and authenticity can be validated without relying solely on external protocols like TLS or DTLS. For real-time systems that operate in sensitive or hostile environments, such as industrial control systems or military communications, this embedded layer of security provides a valuable defense against common threats.

Despite these advantages, SCTP has faced challenges in widespread adoption, primarily due to limitations in network infrastructure and middleware support. Firewalls and NAT devices, often configured to expect only TCP or UDP traffic, may block or mishandle SCTP packets. This has historically restricted its deployment to specialized environments, such as telecom signaling systems and specific high-reliability networks. However, as support for SCTP improves in operating systems, development frameworks, and tunneling solutions like SCTP-over-UDP, its accessibility and practical viability continue to grow.

Ultimately, in real-time contexts, SCTP offers a compelling alternative to both TCP and UDP by addressing their critical shortcomings while preserving their useful features. Its architecture supports the essential needs of latency-sensitive, reliability-demanding, and high-availability applications. As the digital landscape evolves to include increasingly complex and demanding use cases, SCTP stands ready to serve as a transport protocol that combines efficiency, robustness, and intelligence at the core of real-time communication systems.

Multi-Streaming and Its Importance

Multi-streaming is one of the defining innovations of the Stream Control Transmission Protocol, designed to overcome the limitations inherent in traditional transport layer protocols like TCP. In real-time communication systems, the ability to handle multiple independent streams of data within a single connection is not just a technical improvement but a necessity. Multi-streaming fundamentally alters how applications interact with the transport layer by introducing concurrency, reducing latency, and mitigating the effects of transmission delays. This architectural advancement has profound implications for performance, reliability, and user experience in networked systems where diverse types of data need to flow simultaneously without interference.

In conventional TCP connections, all data transmitted is part of a single, ordered stream. TCP enforces strict in-order delivery, meaning that if one segment is lost or delayed, all subsequent segments must wait until the missing data is recovered and processed. This behavior, known as head-of-line blocking, becomes especially problematic in real-time and multimedia applications where different types of data have different priorities and tolerance for delay. A single delayed packet, even if it belongs to a low-priority message, can prevent time-sensitive data like voice or video from being delivered promptly. This serialized processing model introduces inefficiencies and can degrade the quality of service, leading to jitter, dropped frames, or a choppy audio experience.

SCTP introduces multi-streaming to solve this problem. Within a single SCTP association, multiple logical streams can be created, each with its own sequence of Transmission Sequence Numbers, or TSNs. These streams are independently managed by the protocol, allowing messages from different streams to be delivered to the application as soon as they are received, without being blocked by delays in other streams. This architectural separation ensures that real-time data can maintain its timeliness and that less critical information does not interfere with the delivery of high-priority content. By decoupling the sequencing of messages between streams, SCTP allows for parallel data flow that aligns much more closely with the actual needs of modern applications.

The benefits of multi-streaming become even more apparent in applications with complex data structures or multiple communication channels. For instance, a video conferencing system typically handles audio, video, chat messages, control signals, and screen sharing simultaneously. Each of these channels has different delivery requirements. Audio needs to be low-latency and relatively tolerant to occasional losses, while video may require more bandwidth and buffering. Control messages, such as mute commands or layout changes, need to be delivered reliably and quickly to maintain synchronization across participants. Without multi-streaming, all this data would have to share a single stream, resulting in potential delays and resource contention. With SCTP, each type of data can be assigned its own stream, ensuring that a delay or retransmission in one does not disrupt the others.

From a development standpoint, multi-streaming also simplifies application logic. In TCP, developers often have to implement complex protocols at the application layer to simulate stream separation, reassemble messages, or prioritize data. These workarounds can be error-prone, inefficient, and inconsistent across implementations. SCTP offloads this burden to the transport layer, where stream management is handled transparently and efficiently. Applications can focus on delivering functionality rather than compensating for limitations in the underlying protocol. This design encourages cleaner architectures, faster development cycles, and more reliable systems.

In high-performance computing environments and distributed systems, multi-streaming contributes to throughput optimization. By parallelizing data delivery and eliminating unnecessary serialization, SCTP enables better utilization of available bandwidth. Multiple data flows can be transmitted simultaneously without waiting for the completion or acknowledgment of other streams. This concurrent transmission model not only improves overall data rates but also reduces the perceived latency experienced by end users. As network speeds increase and applications become more data-intensive, the ability to manage multiple streams efficiently becomes critical to maintaining responsive and scalable systems.

Another dimension of multi-streaming's importance lies in its role in fault isolation and error recovery. Because each stream is independently sequenced, errors or retransmissions in one stream do not compromise the integrity of others. This containment reduces the impact of packet loss and simplifies recovery procedures. In contrast, TCP must halt the entire data flow until missing data is recovered, regardless of its content or importance. SCTP's selective acknowledgment mechanism further enhances this capability by enabling precise retransmission of lost messages within the affected stream, without burdening unrelated streams. This selective handling leads to more efficient error recovery and minimizes unnecessary retransmissions, conserving bandwidth and reducing congestion.

Multi-streaming also has implications for security and resilience. In critical systems such as military networks, emergency communications, or financial trading platforms, predictable and isolated data flow is essential. Assigning different types of messages to separate streams within the same secure association allows for better control and monitoring. If anomalous behavior is detected in one stream, it can be managed or isolated without affecting the overall session. Moreover, the ability to maintain multiple communication channels within a single association reduces the number of connections that must be established and secured, simplifying encryption and authentication processes while lowering the attack surface.

The real-time nature of modern applications demands a transport protocol that can match their complexity and responsiveness. Multistreaming gives SCTP a decisive advantage in environments where concurrent data flows must be maintained with precision and speed. It reflects a design philosophy that embraces concurrency and modularity rather than fighting against it. As applications continue to evolve toward greater interactivity and data diversity, the need for efficient stream management will only become more pronounced.

SCTP's implementation of multi-streaming is a powerful demonstration of how protocol-level innovation can directly influence application performance and user satisfaction. It eliminates a class of problems that have long plagued TCP-based systems and provides a clean, robust solution that aligns with the architecture of contemporary networked applications. Whether in multimedia platforms, signaling networks, or industrial control systems, the advantages of multi-streaming manifest in smoother operation, higher reliability, and a better end-user experience. This feature, more than any other, highlights SCTP's forward-thinking design and its readiness to serve as a foundational element in the next generation of transport protocols.

Multi-Homing for Fault Tolerance

One of the most significant architectural advantages of the Stream Control Transmission Protocol is its support for multi-homing, a feature that offers a powerful approach to fault tolerance and network resilience. In the context of SCTP, multi-homing refers to the ability of each endpoint in an association to be represented by more than one IP address. This design allows an SCTP-enabled host to be connected to multiple networks or interfaces simultaneously, providing redundant communication paths between the two peers. Unlike traditional transport layer protocols like TCP and UDP, which operate over a single source and destination IP address, SCTP was designed from the ground up to enable automatic failover and increased reliability without requiring complex intervention from higher layers.

The essence of multi-homing in SCTP lies in its capacity to detect path failures and reroute traffic through alternate routes without disrupting the ongoing session. Each SCTP association designates a primary path for normal communication, but it also maintains knowledge of additional paths through which data can be sent if necessary. These alternative paths are verified and monitored using periodic heartbeat messages. Should the primary path become unavailable due to link failure, congestion, or any other network disruption, SCTP can seamlessly redirect traffic through one of the backup paths. This switchover occurs transparently to the application, preserving session continuity and avoiding the costly process of tearing down and re-establishing a new connection.

This level of built-in redundancy provides a significant improvement over the behavior of TCP. In a TCP session, a path failure typically results in a dropped connection, requiring the application to recognize the failure and attempt to reconnect. In many systems, this can cause service interruptions, data loss, or increased latency. SCTP's ability to maintain session integrity across multiple network interfaces greatly enhances fault tolerance, making it especially valuable in mission-critical and real-time applications. Environments such as financial trading platforms, emergency response systems, and industrial automation systems cannot afford delays caused by connection resets or network downtime. With SCTP, these systems gain the robustness necessary to operate under variable and unpredictable network conditions.

The benefits of multi-homing are not limited to redundancy. They also extend to improved load distribution and performance optimization. In certain configurations, it is possible to implement advanced path management techniques where traffic can be distributed across multiple available paths, based on bandwidth availability, latency, or other performance metrics. While basic SCTP behavior uses a single path for transmission, extended features and custom implementations can allow for load-aware routing. This capability opens the door for optimized resource utilization and improved quality of service, particularly in complex networks where different paths exhibit different characteristics.

Multi-homing also supports the dynamic reconfiguration of network paths. SCTP allows endpoints to add or remove IP addresses from an existing association during its lifetime. This dynamic address reconfiguration, managed through specific control chunks, enables devices to adapt to changes in network topology, such as those caused by mobility or interface changes. A mobile device switching from a Wi-Fi network to a cellular network, for instance, can continue its SCTP session without interruption by simply updating its list of valid IP addresses. This feature is especially beneficial in modern, heterogeneous environments where mobility and multi-interface connectivity are becoming standard.

Another key advantage of SCTP's multi-homing is its contribution to increased network security and robustness against certain types of attacks. By allowing communication over multiple paths, the protocol reduces reliance on any single point of failure. Attackers attempting to disrupt communication by targeting a specific network link may find it more difficult to succeed when SCTP is in use, as the protocol can automatically switch to a different, unaffected path. Additionally, multi-homing provides an opportunity for implementing policies that selectively route sensitive traffic over more secure or trusted networks while relegating less critical data to public or less secure channels. This capability is useful in government, military, and enterprise environments with strict segmentation requirements.

Despite its technical strengths, implementing multi-homing introduces certain complexities, particularly in terms of address management, routing policies, and interaction with intermediate network devices. For instance, firewalls and network address translation devices must be configured to understand and accommodate SCTP's use of multiple source and destination addresses. Traditional NAT behavior, which is optimized for TCP and UDP, may interfere with SCTP's handshake or failover mechanisms unless proper SCTP-aware configurations or middleboxes are deployed. This aspect has historically posed a barrier to SCTP's widespread deployment on the open internet, although within controlled networks or specialized environments, the benefits of multi-homing often outweigh the setup challenges.

The overhead associated with maintaining multiple network paths is another consideration. Heartbeat messages, which are sent periodically to verify the status of alternative paths, add additional traffic to the network. While this overhead is generally minimal, it must be accounted for in systems with extremely tight performance or bandwidth constraints. Proper configuration of heartbeat intervals and retransmission strategies can help balance the need for responsiveness with the goal of minimizing unnecessary traffic.

Furthermore, the decision logic for path failover is a critical part of SCTP's multi-homing architecture. The protocol defines thresholds for missed heartbeats before declaring a path unreachable, but these settings may need to be tuned based on specific network conditions or application requirements. A failover that occurs too quickly may respond to transient packet loss, while one that occurs too slowly might cause unnecessary delay in recovering from actual failures. The flexibility of SCTP allows for such tuning, but it also places responsibility on implementers to understand the characteristics of their network and configure parameters appropriately.

Multi-homing as implemented in SCTP is more than a redundancy mechanism; it is a comprehensive fault-tolerance strategy embedded at the transport layer. It addresses both reliability and adaptability by allowing endpoints to maintain robust associations across diverse and dynamic network infrastructures. For developers and network engineers, understanding how to leverage SCTP's multi-homing capabilities opens the door to building systems that remain connected and operational even under adverse conditions. In scenarios where continuity of service is paramount and where the cost of disconnection is high, SCTP offers a powerful solution that traditional protocols cannot easily replicate. The integration of path diversity, dynamic reconfiguration, and automatic failover into a single cohesive protocol makes SCTP uniquely suited to meet the demands of contemporary real-time and critical network applications.

Four-Way Handshake: SCTP Association Setup

The process of establishing communication between two endpoints is fundamental to any transport protocol, and in the case of the Stream Control Transmission Protocol, this process is defined by a unique and robust four-way handshake. Unlike TCP's widely known three-way handshake, which has been the standard for decades, SCTP's association setup was intentionally designed to address critical shortcomings in TCP's approach, particularly its vulnerability to certain types of denial-of-service attacks and the inefficiencies associated with premature allocation of system resources. The four-way handshake used by SCTP provides a more secure and deliberate method of initializing communication between peers, reflecting the protocol's focus on reliability, security, and resilience.

In the SCTP model, a connection is not referred to as a session or a connection, as it is in TCP, but rather as an association. An association is established between two endpoints, each of which may be associated with multiple IP addresses thanks to SCTP's support for multi-homing. Before data can be exchanged over this association, both endpoints must participate in a carefully coordinated series of message exchanges that validate the integrity of the connection request and allocate system resources only when the legitimacy of the initiating party has been established.

The four-way handshake begins when the initiating endpoint, known as the client, sends an INIT chunk to the intended recipient, the server. This INIT chunk contains a variety of information, including a Verification Tag, an Initial Transmission Sequence Number (TSN), and parameters such as the number of outbound streams the client supports. The Verification Tag is a crucial element, serving as a security token that must match in subsequent messages to ensure the continuity and authenticity of the session. Importantly, the reception of the INIT chunk does not immediately cause the server to allocate any significant resources, which is a major departure from the behavior of TCP. Instead, the server responds by generating a cryptographic cookie, encapsulating state information about the proposed association, and sending it back to the client in a COOKIE-ECHO chunk.

This use of a cookie mechanism is a direct mitigation against SYN flooding attacks, a common exploit that targets TCP's vulnerability to overcommit resources during the initial handshake. In TCP, a server allocates memory and maintains half-open connections upon receiving the first SYN packet, leading to potential exhaustion of system resources if multiple fake requests are sent. SCTP avoids this by postponing any stateful commitment until the third step of its handshake, ensuring that the server only stores state information for clients who demonstrate their legitimacy by returning the correct cookie. The cookie itself is generated using a keyed hash or other secure method, tying it to the server's current state in a way that cannot be easily guessed or forged by an attacker.

When the client receives the INIT-ACK chunk containing the cookie, it responds with a COOKIE-ECHO chunk, sending the server's cookie back without alteration. This message signals that the client has received the server's reply and is willing to proceed with the association. The cookie's content allows the server to reconstruct the state of the original INIT request without needing to maintain session information in memory between the INIT and COOKIE-ECHO messages. This approach greatly enhances the scalability of servers under high-load conditions, as it dramatically reduces the window of vulnerability to resource-based attacks.

Upon receiving the COOKIE-ECHO chunk, the server validates the cookie using its internal secrets and, if the validation is successful, allocates the necessary resources and responds with a final COOKIE-ACK chunk. At this point, the association is fully established, and both parties may begin transmitting data. Unlike TCP, where a connection is considered active after the third step, SCTP's handshake does not consider the association complete until the fourth and final message is exchanged. This additional layer of verification ensures that only valid and responsive endpoints are allowed to initiate communication, reinforcing SCTP's reputation as a transport protocol built with security and robustness in mind.

The four-way handshake also introduces a measure of symmetry and fairness into the connection establishment process. By requiring mutual exchange and validation of identity and state information, SCTP avoids the unilateral commitment of resources that can occur in TCP. Each side has an opportunity to assess the other before finalizing the association, enabling better control and awareness of the communication context. This symmetry is especially important in distributed systems where endpoints may dynamically change their roles and where both parties must maintain high levels of trust and coordination.

Moreover, the design of the four-way handshake facilitates cleaner integration of advanced features such as authentication and encryption. SCTP supports extensions that allow for the inclusion of message authentication codes, enabling both peers to validate the integrity and origin of handshake messages. These capabilities enhance the trustworthiness of the association setup process and are especially valuable in environments where security is a top priority, such as in signaling networks for telecommunications or in control systems for infrastructure management.

Another advantage of SCTP's four-way handshake is its compatibility with multi-homing and its ability to gather path information early in the communication process. During the exchange of INIT and INIT-ACK chunks, both endpoints share their lists of available IP addresses. This early discovery allows SCTP to begin path validation and selection procedures even before user data is sent. The subsequent heartbeat mechanism can then be activated immediately following the handshake, ensuring that alternate paths are monitored for availability from the outset of the association.

The deliberate structure of the SCTP handshake offers clear benefits for application developers and system architects. It provides a well-defined and secure mechanism for association setup that can be reliably implemented across a wide range of systems. Because the handshake process is deterministic and avoids ambiguous transitional states, debugging and diagnostics are easier, and the behavior of the protocol remains predictable even under conditions of network loss or delay.

In high-availability applications, the ability to recover from partial handshake failures is also valuable. For example, if a COOKIE-ECHO is lost in transit, the client can retransmit it without restarting the entire handshake. Similarly, because the server does not retain state information after sending the INIT-ACK, it is protected against repeated requests from the same source unless the correct cookie is returned, ensuring that only legitimate requests are honored.

The SCTP four-way handshake stands as a carefully engineered improvement over traditional connection establishment protocols. Its focus on verification, resource protection, and resilience underpins many of the protocol's advantages in real-world deployments. From protecting against attacks to ensuring seamless initialization across multiple paths, the SCTP handshake serves as a model of how modern transport protocols can enhance both performance and security by design.

Chunk-Based Message Structure

The Stream Control Transmission Protocol introduces a novel and flexible approach to data transmission through its chunk-based message structure. Unlike traditional transport protocols that either use a stream of bytes, as in TCP, or a simple datagram format like UDP, SCTP organizes all communication into discrete units known as chunks. This fundamental design decision impacts every aspect of SCTP's functionality, from connection setup and data transmission to error handling and protocol extension. The chunk-based structure allows SCTP to efficiently manage complex associations, accommodate a variety of control messages, and support extensibility while maintaining consistency and modularity across its implementation.

An SCTP packet, the basic transmission unit of the protocol, consists of a common header followed by one or more chunks. The common header contains information that applies to the entire packet, such as the source and destination ports, a verification tag for association validation, and a checksum used for error detection. Following this header, the body of the packet is filled with chunks, each with its own type, length, flags, and optional data fields. The chunks are processed independently, allowing multiple control and data functions to be executed within a single transmission, thereby reducing overhead and improving efficiency.

There are two main categories of chunks in SCTP: control chunks and data chunks. Control chunks are used for managing the state and behavior of the association. They include types such as INIT, INIT-ACK, COOKIE-ECHO, COOKIE-ACK, SHUTDOWN, ABORT, and HEARTBEAT. Each of these serves a specific role in the association lifecycle, from initiation and maintenance to graceful termination and failure recovery. The modular design of chunks means that new control messages can be introduced to the protocol without disrupting existing functionality. This extensibility is one of the key advantages of SCTP's architecture and has allowed the protocol to evolve over time to meet new requirements and use cases.

Data chunks, on the other hand, are responsible for carrying the actual user data. Each data chunk includes a Transmission Sequence Number, or TSN, which is used to ensure reliable and ordered delivery within a stream. It also includes stream identifiers and sequence numbers that enable SCTP's multi-streaming capability. Because each data chunk is a self-contained unit with all necessary metadata for delivery and sequencing, SCTP can handle parallel streams within the same association without interference or the risk of head-of-line blocking. This level of granularity and control is simply not available in protocols like TCP, where sequencing is handled at the byte level and is shared across the entire connection.

The chunk-based format also simplifies retransmissions and error handling. When a packet is lost or corrupted, SCTP does not need to resend the entire set of data from the lost point forward, as TCP typically does. Instead, it can selectively retransmit only the missing chunks, as identified by the receiving endpoint through SACK (Selective Acknowledgment) chunks. These acknowledgment chunks list the TSNs that have been successfully received, as well as any gaps in the sequence. This fine-grained feedback mechanism enables more efficient use of bandwidth and reduces the time required to recover from transmission errors.

Another advantage of the chunk-based structure is its role in supporting partial reliability. Through the Partial Reliability Extension (PR-SCTP), the protocol allows certain data chunks to be sent with expiration conditions. If the data cannot be delivered within a specified time or before a particular event occurs, it can be discarded rather than retransmitted. This behavior is particularly useful in real-time applications where late data is no longer useful. The ability to define such policies at the chunk level empowers developers to make trade-offs between reliability and timeliness, tailoring behavior to the specific needs of their applications.

SCTP also uses chunks to manage heartbeats and monitor the health of network paths in multi-homed environments. Heartbeat chunks are sent periodically to alternate paths to verify their availability. If acknowledgments are not received within a configured threshold, the path is marked as inactive. This continuous monitoring allows SCTP to perform seamless failovers and maintain association integrity even when parts of the network become unavailable. All of this logic is encapsulated within a standardized set of chunks, ensuring interoperability and predictability across implementations.

The use of chunks extends beyond operational control and data transmission to include security and authentication. For example, SCTP supports the use of AUTH chunks, which carry message authentication codes that verify the integrity and authenticity of other chunks in the packet. This built-in support for authentication enhances SCTP's resistance to spoofing and tampering, providing a level of security that is not inherently available in TCP or UDP. Because these AUTH chunks are integrated into the protocol's native structure, they are both efficient and consistent with the rest of SCTP's operation.

From a development perspective, the chunk-based structure promotes clarity and modularity in protocol implementation. Developers can focus on handling specific chunk types independently, facilitating easier debugging, testing, and maintenance. The separation of concerns inherent in chunk processing mirrors modern software engineering practices, where modular components are preferred for their scalability and ease of integration. As new use cases emerge and as SCTP is extended to support additional features, such as advanced congestion control mechanisms or improved mobility support, new chunk types can be introduced without redesigning the protocol's core.

Network engineers also benefit from the chunk structure when performing diagnostics or traffic analysis. Tools such as Wireshark are able to dissect SCTP packets with precision, identifying individual chunks and interpreting their contents. This visibility allows for more accurate troubleshooting, performance optimization, and security auditing. When analyzing TCP traffic, much of the application-layer data must be reconstructed from a continuous stream, whereas SCTP's message boundaries and chunk identifiers provide immediate context for each part of the communication.

In dynamic and heterogeneous networking environments, the flexibility afforded by SCTP's chunk-based structure becomes a strategic advantage. Whether managing multiple streams, handling partial reliability, or executing fast failovers, each operation is driven by one or more chunks tailored to that purpose. The clear delineation between chunk types enables a high degree of control and adaptability, making SCTP particularly well suited for systems where requirements can shift rapidly, such as mobile networks, multimedia platforms, and industrial control systems.

The chunk-based message structure of SCTP is not merely an implementation detail but a foundational aspect of the protocol's identity. It supports a level of extensibility, modularity, and precision that is unmatched in older transport layer protocols. Every chunk serves a defined role, and their collective orchestration allows SCTP to deliver a transport service that is not only reliable and secure but also versatile and future-proof. This structural choice empowers SCTP to support a broad range of applications and network architectures, from telecommunications signaling to real-time streaming, all while maintaining consistency and performance across diverse environments.

Data Transfer Mechanisms in SCTP

The Stream Control Transmission Protocol was designed to address many of the limitations found in earlier transport protocols, particularly those related to the transmission of data across complex and evolving network environments. The mechanisms it employs for data transfer are central to its ability to deliver robust, reliable, and adaptable communication, particularly in real-time and mission-critical contexts. These mechanisms are not only more advanced than those in TCP and UDP but are also designed to support a wider range of applications by providing granular control, efficiency, and error resilience. Understanding how SCTP handles data transfer sheds light on why it is such a powerful tool for modern networking.

At the core of SCTP's data transfer architecture lies the concept of message orientation. Unlike TCP, which treats data as a continuous stream of bytes, SCTP preserves the boundaries of messages, ensuring that each message sent by the sender is received intact and without fragmentation at the receiver. This preservation is particularly valuable for signaling and transactional applications where each unit of data carries a distinct meaning. The ability to maintain message integrity at the transport layer simplifies application development and avoids the need for additional logic to reassemble messages that may have been split across multiple packets in transit.

Data in SCTP is transferred using data chunks, each of which carries a discrete piece of user data along with metadata necessary for proper sequencing, reliability, and stream identification. Every data chunk contains a Transmission Sequence Number, or TSN, which is globally unique within the association and is used to track and acknowledge received data. This TSN system allows SCTP to ensure that all data is delivered reliably and in order within each stream, even when the underlying network is lossy or disordered. Furthermore, each data chunk includes a Stream Identifier and a Stream Sequence Number, which enable the protocol's multi-streaming capability, allowing multiple independent sequences of data to be transmitted simultaneously within the same association.

SCTP uses selective acknowledgments to enhance reliability and efficiency in data transfer. Rather than acknowledging each individual data chunk or using cumulative acknowledgments like TCP, SCTP implements the Selective Acknowledgment (SACK) mechanism. SACK chunks report all received data chunks, including any gaps in the TSN sequence. This allows the sender to retransmit only the missing chunks rather than guessing which data might have been lost. The result is a more efficient use of network resources, reduced retransmission traffic, and faster recovery from packet loss.

To further optimize the data transfer process, SCTP includes mechanisms for bundling multiple chunks into a single packet. This bundling capability reduces the overhead associated with header fields and can improve transmission efficiency, especially in scenarios where small control messages must be sent alongside user data. For example, a SACK chunk and a data chunk can be transmitted together, reducing the number of packets that must be exchanged and improving the responsiveness of the association.

Congestion control is another key component of SCTP's data transfer mechanisms. SCTP employs a congestion control strategy that is inspired by TCP but adapted to support the protocol's unique features such as multi-homing and multi-streaming. It includes congestion window management, slow start, and congestion avoidance algorithms to ensure fair and efficient use of the network. However, SCTP enhances this model by allowing independent congestion control per destination address in multi-homed associations. This means that each path can be evaluated and adjusted independently, allowing SCTP to route more traffic through less congested paths while reducing traffic on congested ones. This per-path congestion control helps optimize data delivery in networks where multiple paths between endpoints exist, thereby improving overall performance and reliability.

Flow control is similarly essential in maintaining balanced and stable communication. SCTP uses a receiver-advertised window to manage flow control, ensuring that the sender does not overwhelm the receiver with more data than it can process. The receiver continuously informs the sender of how much buffer space is available, and the sender respects these limits by throttling its data transmission accordingly. This process prevents buffer overflows and promotes fairness between multiple associations sharing the same system resources.

In situations where data cannot be delivered in time to be useful, SCTP offers partial reliability through the Partial Reliability Extension (PR-SCTP). This allows the sender to specify conditions under which certain data chunks should be abandoned instead of being endlessly retransmitted. Conditions might include time limits, retransmission limits, or application-layer requests. This capability is especially useful in real-time communication scenarios where old data is no longer useful if delayed, such as in live audio or video streams. By discarding stale data, SCTP avoids wasting bandwidth and reduces latency, improving the quality of service in applications where timely delivery is more important than guaranteed delivery.

Another key element in SCTP's data transfer is path management. In multi-homed associations, SCTP continuously monitors the health of each available path using heartbeat chunks. If a path fails, the protocol automatically switches to a healthy alternative without disrupting the ongoing data transfer. This seamless transition is crucial for maintaining uninterrupted communication in environments where network conditions change frequently or where high availability is required. Path management and dynamic path selection not only enhance fault tolerance but also contribute to improved load balancing and traffic distribution.

The chunk-based data transfer model of SCTP also supports advanced features like message interleaving, which allows the interleaving of messages from different streams to avoid head-of-line blocking even within a single stream. This feature, which is an extension of the base protocol, is especially valuable in scenarios involving large messages or high-priority interactive traffic mixed with bulk transfers. By breaking down large messages into fragments and allowing those fragments to be interleaved with smaller, time-sensitive messages, SCTP provides an even finer level of control over the delivery process.

The reliability of data delivery in SCTP is further strengthened by its robust retransmission timeout mechanisms. These timers are dynamically adjusted based on round-trip time measurements to balance responsiveness with stability. If acknowledgments are not received within the expected timeframe, retransmissions are triggered, ensuring that data is eventually delivered despite transient network issues. These timers are carefully managed to avoid unnecessary retransmissions while still ensuring timely recovery from loss.

In SCTP, every aspect of data transfer is designed to maximize control, reliability, and adaptability. From its message-oriented structure and multi-streaming support to its selective acknowledgment and per-path congestion control, the protocol embodies a comprehensive approach to modern data transport. These mechanisms work in concert to provide a transport service capable of supporting the diverse and demanding requirements of real-time, high-availability, and secure applications across a broad range of network environments.

Congestion Control Strategies

The Stream Control Transmission Protocol employs a suite of congestion control strategies that draw inspiration from TCP while introducing enhancements tailored to SCTP's unique features such as multi-homing and multi-streaming. At its core, the purpose of congestion control is to ensure fair and efficient utilization of network resources, prevent network collapse due to excessive traffic, and adapt to changing conditions in real-time. These goals become especially important in environments where SCTP is used to support latency-sensitive applications, such as real-time communications, signaling systems, and live data feeds. The mechanisms SCTP uses to manage congestion are dynamic, adaptive, and carefully calibrated to maintain a balance between throughput and stability.

SCTP begins congestion control with the same basic principle as TCP: avoid overwhelming the network and the receiver. To achieve this, SCTP introduces a congestion window, or cwnd, which limits the amount of unacknowledged data that can be in flight at any given time. This window adjusts over time based on feedback from the receiver and the observed behavior of the network. The size of the congestion window is initially small and grows as acknowledgments are received successfully, allowing the sender to increase its sending rate. This process, known as slow start, is designed to probe the network gradually to discover its available capacity without causing sudden spikes in traffic that could lead to packet loss.

During the slow start phase, SCTP doubles the congestion window each round-trip time, rapidly increasing throughput until a loss is detected or a threshold is reached. At that point, the protocol transitions into congestion avoidance mode. In this phase, the growth of the congestion window becomes more conservative, typically increasing linearly rather than exponentially. This strategy helps to stabilize traffic flow and maintain high throughput while minimizing the risk of congestion. If packet loss is detected, SCTP interprets it as a sign of network congestion and reacts by reducing the size of the congestion window, thereby decreasing the sending rate to alleviate pressure on the network.

A critical distinction in SCTP's congestion control approach is its support for multi-homing. Each SCTP association can involve multiple network paths, and the protocol maintains separate congestion control variables for each path. This per-destination congestion control allows SCTP to adapt its behavior based on the characteristics of each individual path. For instance, if one path exhibits signs of congestion, the protocol can reduce its sending rate on that path while continuing normal transmission on other, uncongested paths. This approach provides a more nuanced and responsive way to handle varying network conditions, improving both efficiency and resilience. It also enables SCTP to perform load balancing across paths, maximizing bandwidth usage while avoiding overloading any single route.

Selective acknowledgments play a vital role in SCTP's congestion control strategies. By receiving detailed information about which chunks have been successfully delivered and which are missing, the sender can make informed decisions about retransmissions and window adjustments. The use of SACKs reduces unnecessary retransmissions and allows the sender to maintain a more accurate view of the network state. This granularity enhances the precision of congestion control actions, allowing for quicker recovery and smoother adjustments.

Retransmission timeouts are another key element in SCTP's congestion control toolkit. If an acknowledgment for a data chunk is not received within a certain time, the sender assumes the chunk was lost and retransmits it. The timeout value is not fixed but is dynamically adjusted based on round-trip time measurements. This adaptability helps prevent premature or excessive retransmissions that could exacerbate congestion. When a retransmission timeout occurs, SCTP reduces the congestion window significantly, often back to the initial value, and re-enters slow start to cautiously rebuild transmission speed. This cautious approach is essential in maintaining network stability, particularly in shared or variable environments where conditions can change rapidly.

To further refine its congestion control behavior, SCTP implements a mechanism called fast retransmit and fast recovery. When the sender receives a certain number of duplicate SACKs indicating that a chunk has not been received but subsequent data has been, it can infer that the chunk was lost. Rather than waiting for a timeout, the sender can retransmit the missing chunk immediately. This early intervention helps maintain throughput and reduces delays caused by waiting for a full timeout. After performing a fast retransmit, SCTP enters fast recovery mode, adjusting the congestion window to reflect the presumed state of the network and allowing transmission to continue at a reduced rate.

The interplay between flow control and congestion control is also carefully managed in SCTP. Flow control ensures that the sender does not transmit more data than the receiver can handle, while congestion control focuses on the network's capacity. Both mechanisms use window sizes to regulate transmission, but they operate independently. The sender must honor both the flow control window advertised by the receiver and the congestion window determined by its own algorithms. This dual-window system ensures that neither the receiver nor the network becomes a bottleneck or a point of failure.

SCTP's congestion control strategies are particularly effective in heterogeneous and high-mobility networks, such as mobile or satellite links, where latency and packet loss can vary significantly. Traditional TCP congestion control mechanisms often misinterpret non-congestion-related packet loss as a sign of congestion, resulting in unnecessary throttling. SCTP, through its use of separate congestion control per path and detailed acknowledgment mechanisms, is better equipped to distinguish between congestion and other causes of packet loss, leading to more appropriate responses and better performance.

Emerging extensions to SCTP continue to enhance its congestion control capabilities. For example, the addition of message interleaving allows large user messages to be broken into smaller chunks and interleaved with other traffic, minimizing the delay introduced by single-stream congestion. This fine-grained control allows for smoother handling of mixed traffic types and provides another tool for managing network congestion intelligently.

SCTP's architecture anticipates the demands of future networks by integrating sophisticated, adaptive congestion control strategies that respond effectively to real-world conditions. Its design reflects a deep understanding of the complexities of network behavior and a commitment to building systems that are both efficient and resilient. Whether in high-speed terrestrial networks or bandwidth-constrained satellite links, SCTP's congestion control ensures that data flows remain stable, fair, and responsive to the environment. Its mechanisms are not just reactive but proactive, enabling the protocol to perform well under pressure and to deliver consistent quality of service even in the face of fluctuating traffic demands and unpredictable network behavior.

Flow Control and Buffer Management

Flow control and buffer management are essential mechanisms in the Stream Control Transmission Protocol, playing a crucial role in ensuring reliable and efficient data transmission between endpoints. These features are designed to prevent the sender from overwhelming the receiver by regulating the volume of in-flight data based on the receiver's capacity to process and store it. In environments where bandwidth, memory, and processing power vary significantly, the ability of SCTP to dynamically manage these aspects ensures that communication remains stable, fair, and responsive to changing conditions. SCTP's approach to flow control, combined with a careful buffer management strategy, results in a transport protocol that is well-suited to real-time and high-performance applications.

At the center of SCTP's flow control mechanism is the concept of a receiver window. This window indicates how much data the receiver can currently accept without risking buffer overflow. When an association is established, each endpoint allocates buffer space for incoming data. The receiver then advertises the size of its available buffer to the sender by including the value in control chunks such as SACKs. As data is received and processed, the receiver updates the size of this window, enabling the sender to adjust its transmission rate accordingly. This dynamic feedback loop prevents the sender from transmitting more data than the receiver can handle, thus avoiding packet drops and unnecessary retransmissions.

SCTP manages flow control on a per-association basis rather than on a per-stream basis. This means that while data may be distributed across multiple streams, the total volume of in-flight data is controlled globally within the context of the association. This approach simplifies the management of shared resources and ensures fairness among streams. However, it also requires careful coordination between the sender's scheduling algorithms and the receiver's buffer allocation strategies to avoid bottlenecks or starvation of lower-priority streams. Applications that utilize SCTP must be designed with this behavior in mind, particularly when transmitting high volumes of data across multiple concurrent streams.

One of the advantages of SCTP's flow control model is its ability to coexist with its congestion control mechanisms without conflict. While congestion control focuses on the capacity of the network to deliver data without packet loss, flow control is concerned with the receiver's ability to accept and store data. These two systems operate independently, yet their coordination is essential to the overall stability of the communication channel. The sender must always consider both the congestion window, which limits data based on network conditions, and the receiver window, which limits data based on receiver capacity. The minimum of these two values dictates the sender's permissible transmission rate at any given time.

Buffer management is the process by which each endpoint allocates, monitors, and frees memory used for storing incoming and outgoing data. In SCTP, effective buffer management is critical not only for performance but also for maintaining the integrity of the flow control system. When the receiver's buffer is full, it advertises a zero window size, signaling the sender to temporarily halt transmission. This condition, known as a zero-window situation, must be handled gracefully to prevent the sender from entering a busy loop or causing timeouts. SCTP includes a mechanism called the zero-window probing feature, which allows the sender to periodically check whether the receiver's buffer has become available again. This feature ensures that communication can resume promptly once resources are freed without requiring a full renegotiation of the association.

On the sending side, buffer management involves tracking which data chunks have been sent but not yet acknowledged, as well as which chunks are candidates for retransmission. The sender must retain unacknowledged data in its buffer until it either receives confirmation of delivery or determines that the data should be abandoned due to expiration policies or application-layer instructions. Efficient use of the send buffer is essential for maximizing throughput and minimizing latency. This includes intelligent scheduling of data chunks across available streams and paths, especially in multi-homed associations where path characteristics may vary significantly.

Buffer sizing is another important consideration. Allocating too little buffer space can lead to frequent window closures and interruptions in the data flow. On the other hand, overly large buffers can result in increased memory usage and higher latency due to excessive queuing. SCTP implementations must strike a balance based on the expected workload and the characteristics of the underlying hardware and operating system. In real-time systems, where predictability and low latency are paramount, buffer sizes are often carefully tuned to ensure that data is delivered promptly without causing resource contention.

The interaction between flow control and retransmission logic also plays a role in SCTP's buffer management. When packet loss is detected, either through timeout or selective acknowledgment, the sender must retransmit the missing data. However, retransmissions consume buffer space and must be scheduled in a way that respects both the congestion and flow control windows. To handle this efficiently, SCTP uses a retransmission queue, where lost chunks are prioritized and re-sent based on the receiver's advertised window and network conditions. This prioritization ensures that the most critical data is retransmitted first, preserving the quality of service for latency-sensitive applications.

In multi-streaming scenarios, the shared flow control window introduces challenges in stream scheduling. The sender must decide which stream's data to transmit next, ensuring that no stream monopolizes the buffer and that all streams receive a fair share of the available bandwidth. Advanced SCTP implementations may use weighted round-robin or priority-based algorithms to manage this scheduling, giving preference to streams carrying time-sensitive or critical data. These strategies are particularly effective in multimedia applications where control messages, audio, and video streams coexist with differing urgency.

Flow control and buffer management in SCTP are not static mechanisms but adaptive processes that respond to real-time conditions. By monitoring acknowledgment patterns, buffer usage, and network performance, SCTP implementations can adjust their behavior to maintain optimal flow. This adaptability is vital in modern network environments where variability is the norm. Whether facing fluctuating bandwidth, temporary congestion, or sudden bursts of data, SCTP's flow control and buffer strategies provide a stable foundation for reliable transport.

These mechanisms also enhance security and resilience. Buffer exhaustion, whether accidental or maliciously induced, can lead to service disruption. By implementing strict flow control and buffer monitoring, SCTP mitigates the risk of such attacks. Additionally, the protocol's ability to reject new data when the buffer is full prevents unauthorized resource consumption and ensures that existing associations maintain their integrity even under stress.

SCTP's approach to flow control and buffer management reflects a mature and deliberate protocol design. It addresses the limitations of older transport protocols while introducing innovations that align with the demands of contemporary applications. These mechanisms are essential not just for maintaining performance but for enabling SCTP to fulfill its role as a transport layer solution capable of supporting a broad range of real-time, high-availability, and fault-tolerant applications across complex network infrastructures.

SCTP Error Detection and Recovery

The ability of a transport protocol to detect and recover from errors is critical to maintaining the integrity, reliability, and robustness of data communication. The Stream Control Transmission Protocol incorporates a comprehensive set of mechanisms for error detection and recovery that are purpose-built to meet the challenges of modern network environments. These mechanisms are essential in supporting the protocol's reliability guarantees, especially in scenarios where packet loss, duplication, reordering, or corruption can occur. SCTP's approach goes beyond traditional error handling by introducing fine-grained control and adaptive strategies that are well-suited to both static and dynamic network conditions.

At the core of SCTP's error detection framework is a powerful integrity check performed using a 32-bit cyclic redundancy check, or CRC32c. This checksum is calculated for every SCTP packet and covers both the common header and all included chunks. It is significantly more robust than the 16-bit checksum used by TCP and UDP, providing improved detection of bit errors and reducing the probability of undetected corruption. When a packet arrives at its destination, the checksum is recalculated and compared against the value in the packet. If the values do not match, the packet is discarded silently, preventing corrupted data from reaching the application. This checksum operation forms the first line of defense in SCTP's error management system.

SCTP also employs a sequence-based model for tracking and verifying the correct delivery of user data. Each data chunk is assigned a Transmission Sequence Number, or TSN, which serves as a unique identifier for that specific piece of data within the context of an association. The receiver uses these TSNs to maintain a record of which chunks have arrived, which are missing, and which may have been duplicated. This information is communicated back to the sender through Selective Acknowledgment, or SACK, chunks. These SACKs provide detailed feedback, including the cumulative TSN acknowledged and any gaps in the received sequence. Unlike TCP's cumulative acknowledgment, SCTP's SACKs allow for selective reporting of missing data, making the recovery process more efficient and reducing the need for unnecessary retransmissions.

When the sender receives a SACK indicating a gap in the TSN sequence, it marks the corresponding chunks for retransmission. However, SCTP is careful to avoid excessive retransmissions that could exacerbate congestion. It uses timers to determine when a chunk should be retransmitted. If a retransmission timeout, or RTO, occurs before a SACK is received, the sender assumes the chunk was lost and initiates a retransmission. The RTO is dynamically calculated based on observed round-trip times, providing a responsive yet conservative strategy for handling timeouts. SCTP also supports fast retransmission, where multiple duplicate SACKs indicating the same missing chunk can trigger an earlier retransmission, bypassing the standard timeout and improving responsiveness to loss.

To support partial reliability in time-sensitive applications, SCTP includes the Partial Reliability Extension, known as PR-SCTP. This extension allows the sender to assign expiration conditions to individual chunks. If a chunk is not acknowledged within a certain timeframe or under specific conditions, the sender may discard it without retransmission. This behavior is valuable in real-time systems where stale data has no value and may degrade the quality of service if transmitted too late. The ability to define delivery priorities and discard policies adds a layer of flexibility to SCTP's error recovery model, enabling it to serve both high-reliability and low-latency use cases effectively.

In addition to handling errors in user data, SCTP is designed to detect and respond to control message errors and association-level failures. Each association is monitored using heartbeat chunks, which are sent periodically over each network path. If a path fails to respond to a series of heartbeats within a configured threshold, it is marked as inactive. SCTP can then shift transmission to an alternate path if available, preserving the continuity of the association. This path failure detection is vital in multi-homed environments where reliability depends on the protocol's ability to adapt to changing network conditions. The combination of heartbeats, retransmission timers, and alternate path selection provides a comprehensive error recovery model that extends beyond individual packets to the level of network infrastructure.

Duplicate chunk detection is another important feature in SCTP's error management strategy. Since networks can deliver duplicate packets due to retransmissions or misconfigurations, SCTP includes logic to identify and discard any duplicated chunks based on their TSNs. This ensures that the application receives each message exactly once, preserving semantic integrity and avoiding the overhead of handling duplicate data at higher layers. The receiver maintains a sliding window of expected TSNs and quickly filters out any data that falls outside the valid range or has already been processed.

SCTP also supports ABORT and ERROR chunks that allow endpoints to report and respond to serious protocol violations or unexpected conditions. An ABORT chunk immediately terminates the association without the graceful shutdown process, typically used when a fatal error is detected. ERROR chunks provide diagnostic feedback, enabling the sender to understand what went wrong and potentially adjust its behavior. These control chunks offer an administrative channel for dealing with anomalies that are not covered by standard retransmission and acknowledgment mechanisms, enhancing the transparency and debuggability of the protocol.

For applications operating in constrained or hostile environments, such as industrial control systems, military communications, or high-security networks, SCTP's error detection and recovery mechanisms offer strong protection against data loss, corruption, and disruption. The ability to maintain data integrity, recover from loss efficiently, and switch paths in the face of failure makes SCTP highly suitable for systems where uptime and data accuracy are non-negotiable. The protocol's structure allows implementers to fine-tune recovery behavior to match the specific needs of their use case, whether that means maximizing reliability, reducing latency, or minimizing bandwidth usage.

From its use of advanced checksums and selective acknowledgments to its dynamic timers, fast retransmit logic, and partial reliability features, SCTP's error handling capabilities represent a significant advancement over older transport layer protocols. It anticipates the wide range of errors that can occur in complex networks and offers tools to detect, report, and recover from them with precision and minimal disruption. This robust error management framework is a cornerstone of SCTP's effectiveness as a modern, adaptable, and resilient transport protocol.

Path Management and Heartbeat Mechanisms

The Stream Control Transmission Protocol was designed with the realities of modern networking in mind, including the prevalence of redundant connections, dynamic route availability, and variable network reliability. One of the most sophisticated features SCTP offers is its native support for multi-homing, which allows endpoints to communicate over multiple network paths simultaneously. To manage these paths effectively, SCTP incorporates a comprehensive path management system that works in conjunction with heartbeat mechanisms to monitor the health of each path and ensure seamless communication continuity. These components together form a critical part of SCTP's resilience and reliability, especially in scenarios where uninterrupted communication is vital.

In SCTP, when an association is established, each endpoint can present a list of IP addresses that represent potential paths for communication. These addresses are exchanged during the initial handshake process, and from that point on, SCTP is aware of all viable paths available to both sides of the association. Among these paths, one is designated as the primary path, which is typically used for sending user data. However, all other paths are considered alternate paths and are monitored in parallel. This arrangement means that if the primary path fails, SCTP can quickly switch to another available path without requiring any intervention from the application layer or causing disruption to the data exchange.

To keep track of the state of each path, SCTP uses heartbeat mechanisms. These are lightweight control messages sent periodically from one endpoint to another along a specific path. The primary purpose of a heartbeat is to verify the operational status of that path. When a heartbeat is sent, the sender expects a corresponding heartbeat acknowledgment, or HEARTBEAT-ACK, to confirm that the path is still active and capable of carrying data. The absence of a timely acknowledgment triggers internal counters and timers within SCTP that help determine whether the path has failed or is experiencing high latency or packet loss.

SCTP implements a configurable threshold for how many consecutive missed heartbeat acknowledgments are allowed before a path is declared inactive. Once this threshold is reached, the path is marked as failed, and SCTP ceases to use it for data transmission. This decision is not permanent; failed paths continue to be probed at longer intervals, allowing for their reactivation if they become operational again. This dynamic monitoring and re-evaluation ensure that SCTP can adapt to fluctuating network conditions, automatically restoring paths when they recover and redistributing traffic as necessary to maintain optimal performance.

When the primary path fails, SCTP automatically promotes one of the available alternate paths to become the new primary. This transition is done seamlessly, preserving the association and continuing data transmission without requiring a reestablishment of the session. This capability is especially important in high-availability applications where network disruptions cannot be allowed to interrupt service. For example, in telecommunication signaling systems or emergency response networks, the ability to reroute data instantly without loss or delay is a critical operational requirement. SCTP meets this need through its integrated path management and heartbeat mechanisms.

The heartbeat interval and the path failure threshold are tunable parameters, allowing administrators and developers to tailor SCTP's behavior to specific use cases. Shorter heartbeat intervals can lead to faster detection of path failures but also increase control traffic and processing overhead. Longer intervals reduce overhead but may delay detection and switchover during outages. Similarly, the number of missed heartbeats tolerated before declaring a path down can be adjusted based on the stability and predictability of the network environment. In stable wired networks, the threshold can be low for quick failover, while in wireless or satellite links, it may be set higher to account for temporary fluctuations.

SCTP's path management system also considers performance characteristics such as round-trip time, congestion, and available bandwidth when managing data transmission. While the protocol does not automatically load balance across multiple paths by default, implementations may include extensions or custom logic to dynamically select the best path for sending data based on real-time performance metrics. By combining path health monitoring with performance assessment, SCTP enables more intelligent and adaptive transmission strategies than traditional single-path protocols like TCP.

In mobile environments, where devices frequently change networks or IP addresses, path management becomes even more critical. SCTP supports dynamic address reconfiguration, allowing endpoints to update their list of reachable addresses during an active association. This feature enables mobile nodes to maintain uninterrupted sessions while roaming between different networks. Heartbeats play a crucial role in this process, as they help verify the viability of newly introduced paths and confirm the failure of those that are no longer reachable. The dynamic nature of SCTP's path management makes it particularly well-suited for mobile applications, vehicular communication systems, and distributed sensor networks.

Another advantage of the heartbeat mechanism is its role in maintaining association liveliness in idle conditions. In cases where no user data is being exchanged, heartbeats serve as a keep-alive signal that ensures the connection remains valid in the eyes of network devices such as firewalls and NATs. This keep-alive function helps prevent premature closure of idle connections and ensures that the association remains available for when data transmission resumes. In some cases, applications can control the use of heartbeats to minimize unnecessary traffic, especially in constrained environments, while still benefiting from SCTP's ability to detect and respond to path failures.

The modularity of SCTP's heartbeat and path management design also aids in security. Because each path is independently monitored, it becomes more difficult for attackers to disrupt communication entirely by targeting a single path. Even if one IP address is attacked or compromised, SCTP can route data through another valid path, maintaining continuity. Furthermore, the use of unique verification tags and strict validation of heartbeats helps prevent spoofed packets from interfering with legitimate path monitoring, adding an additional layer of integrity to the protocol.

From a diagnostic and operational standpoint, SCTP's path management features provide valuable insights into network behavior. Administrators can monitor heartbeat statistics, path failure rates, and switchover events to gain a deeper understanding of network reliability and performance. This visibility can inform decisions about infrastructure upgrades, policy adjustments, or failover strategies in complex systems.

Path management and heartbeat mechanisms in SCTP exemplify the protocol's focus on reliability, adaptability, and operational intelligence. They allow SCTP to monitor, maintain, and optimize multiple communication paths in real-time, ensuring that data continues to flow smoothly even in the face of network instability or disruption. These mechanisms are foundational to SCTP's ability to deliver consistent performance in mission-critical environments, demonstrating the protocol's thoughtful design and its capacity to handle the demands of modern, multi-path communication systems.

SCTP Socket API Programming

Programming with the SCTP socket API requires an understanding of how the protocol extends the conventional socket programming model established by TCP and UDP. SCTP maintains the core design of sockets but introduces a series of enhancements that reflect its multipath, multistream, and message-oriented nature. These features are accessible through specific socket options, data structures, and function calls that expand the standard POSIX socket interface. For developers transitioning from TCP or UDP, SCTP socket programming offers both familiar foundations and unique mechanisms that support its advanced transport features.

The basic process of working with SCTP sockets follows the traditional client-server model. On the server side, a socket is created, bound to an address, set to listen mode, and then used to accept incoming associations. On the client side, a socket is created, and an association is initiated using a connect call. The key distinction lies in the socket type used. While TCP uses SOCK_STREAM and UDP uses SOCK_DGRAM, SCTP allows for both styles depending on the application's needs. The two primary socket types in SCTP are SOCK_STREAM for one-to-one associations and SOCK_SEQPACKET for one-to-many associations. SOCK_SEQPACKET is the more commonly used of the two, offering message-oriented delivery with preservation of message boundaries and supporting multiple associations through a single socket descriptor.

To begin using SCTP, the programmer includes the appropriate header files, such as <netinet/sctp.h>, which define the structures and constants necessary for working with SCTP sockets. Creating a socket is accomplished using the socket function, specifying the protocol family (typically AF_INET or AF_INET6), the socket type (usually SOCK_SEQPACKET), and the protocol identifier for SCTP, which is IPPROTO_SCTP. Once the socket is created, it can be configured with a variety of SCTP-specific options using the setsockopt function. These options enable the developer to control aspects such as stream count, retransmission policies, heartbeat intervals, and authentication parameters.

Binding the socket to one or more IP addresses is an essential step, particularly in multi-homed environments. The standard bind function can be used for simple cases, but SCTP provides an extended function called sctp_bindx, which allows the programmer to bind multiple addresses to a single socket. This capability reflects SCTP's multi-homing design and enables the protocol to manage redundant network paths. The application can specify an array of socket addresses to be associated with the socket, enabling the SCTP stack to perform path selection, monitoring, and failover automatically.

Listening and accepting connections on a server socket follow the usual pattern. The listen function is used to enable incoming connections, and accept is used to handle each new association. When using the one-to-many style with SOCK_SEQPACKET, the recvmsg function is commonly used to receive data along with metadata, such as the source address and stream ID. The SCTP API extends the standard message header structures to include SCTP-specific information through ancillary data. This allows the application to obtain details about the stream, association ID, and message flags, which are necessary for managing the complex interactions that SCTP enables.

Sending and receiving data with SCTP differs from TCP and UDP primarily in the way messages are handled. Because SCTP preserves message boundaries, each call to sendmsg or sctp_sendmsg results in the transmission of a complete message. The application can attach stream identifiers and other flags to each message, allowing fine-grained control over message delivery. For example, by assigning different stream IDs to different types of data, the application can leverage SCTP's multi-streaming feature to prevent head-of-line blocking and maintain responsiveness. The sctp_sendmsg function simplifies this process by allowing stream ID, protocol ID, flags, and destination address to be specified in a single call.

Receiving messages is handled using recvmsg or sctp_recvmsg. These functions provide access to both the payload and the associated metadata, including stream ID and flags indicating whether a message is complete or fragmented. SCTP supports both complete message delivery and partial delivery in cases where large messages must be fragmented across multiple packets. The application must be prepared to handle both scenarios by checking the flags returned by the receive function and managing buffers appropriately. The ability to receive out-of-order messages is also possible, depending on the configuration and stream sequencing rules.

Advanced socket options allow the developer to configure SCTP behavior in detail. For example, the SCTP_INITMSG option can be used to set the number of outbound and inbound streams, the maximum number of initial attempts for association setup, and other parameters related to the establishment phase. The SCTP_EVENTS option enables or disables specific notifications, such as association changes, address changes, send failures, and stream resets. These events are delivered through the same socket as normal data, using the recvmsg function with ancillary data to distinguish them. Handling these notifications is vital for maintaining a responsive and aware application, especially in systems where network conditions may change dynamically.

SCTP also supports the ability to reset streams within an active association. This feature allows the application to clear the sequencing state of a stream without tearing down the entire association, freeing up stream IDs and avoiding stale sequence numbers. The stream reset mechanism is accessible through socket options such as SCTP_STREAM_RESET, which can be used to initiate and respond to reset requests. Proper management of stream resets requires awareness of the state transitions and acknowledgment process defined in the protocol.

Security features in the SCTP socket API include support for message authentication. By using the SCTP_AUTHENTICATION option, the application can configure which chunks must be authenticated and establish shared keys for HMAC-based validation. This capability enhances the integrity of control and data messages and is essential in environments where trust and verification are critical.

Timeouts, retransmission limits, and partial reliability are also configurable through the socket interface. With the SCTP_PR_SCTP policy, the developer can specify expiration times or retransmission caps for individual messages. This level of control allows applications to prioritize real-time constraints over reliability when appropriate, giving SCTP the flexibility to support use cases ranging from file transfer to interactive voice and video.

The SCTP socket API combines traditional socket programming with protocol-specific extensions that expose the full power of SCTP's transport features. It offers developers the tools to build applications that are both robust and adaptable, capable of maintaining high performance and reliability across a wide range of network conditions. Mastery of this API enables precise control over associations, streams, paths, and delivery behavior, making it possible to design communication systems that are secure, efficient, and highly responsive to the needs of modern applications.

Using SCTP in Linux Environments

The Linux operating system provides comprehensive support for the Stream Control Transmission Protocol, making it one of the most practical and accessible platforms for developing and deploying SCTP-based applications. SCTP support in Linux is implemented within the kernel network stack, which means that applications can use standard system calls and libraries to interact with the protocol without requiring specialized user-space components. This native integration allows SCTP to function seamlessly alongside TCP and UDP, taking advantage of the same networking infrastructure while offering advanced features such as multi-homing, multi-streaming, and message-oriented communication. Understanding how to effectively utilize SCTP in a Linux environment involves configuring the operating system, installing the appropriate libraries, and using the correct programming interfaces.

To begin using SCTP on Linux, it is essential to ensure that the kernel supports the protocol. Most modern distributions, including Ubuntu, Debian, Fedora, CentOS, and Arch Linux, include SCTP support by default in the kernel modules. The relevant kernel module is called sctp.ko, and it can be loaded manually using the modprobe command if it is not already active. Administrators can verify SCTP availability by examining the list of loaded modules with lsmod or checking the protocol support in the /proc/net/sctp directory, which provides real-time information about SCTP associations, endpoints, and other statistics.

Once the kernel support is confirmed, developers must ensure that the appropriate header files and libraries are installed for SCTP socket programming. The key library in Linux is the LKSCTP library, which stands for Linux Kernel SCTP. This library provides a user-space API for SCTP and is typically installed using a package manager. For instance, on Debian-based systems, the packages libsctp1 and libsctp-dev provide the runtime and development components, respectively. These packages include the netinet/sctp.h header and allow developers to compile programs that use SCTP-specific socket options, structures, and function calls.

Network configuration is another important step when deploying SCTP in a Linux environment. Multi-homing, one of SCTP's core features, relies on the ability of the system to bind multiple IP addresses to a single interface or to multiple interfaces. This can be accomplished using the ip command from the iproute2 package. Each interface must be configured with a valid IP address, and routing rules must be properly set to ensure that return traffic can reach the intended interface. In production systems, persistent configuration of network interfaces is typically managed through configuration files or network management tools such as Netplan, NetworkManager, or systemd-networkd, depending on the distribution in use.

Firewall configuration is critical for allowing SCTP traffic through the system. Unlike TCP and UDP, SCTP uses its own protocol number, which is 132. Firewall tools such as iptables or nftables must be explicitly configured to allow SCTP traffic on the desired ports. In iptables, this is done by specifying the protocol as sctp using the -p option. For example, allowing SCTP traffic on port 3868 (commonly used for Diameter) would involve a rule like iptables -A INPUT -p sctp --dport 3868 -j ACCEPT. Similar rules must be defined for OUTPUT and FORWARD chains as needed, and these rules should be saved and reloaded on boot to maintain persistent access.

Diagnostic tools in Linux also support SCTP to varying degrees. The ss command, part of the iproute2 suite, can display SCTP sockets and their states using the -P sctp option. The netstat command, though deprecated in many distributions, also supports SCTP if compiled with the appropriate flags. For packet-level analysis, Wireshark is the tool of choice, offering detailed dissection of SCTP packets including INIT, DATA, SACK, and HEARTBEAT chunks. When using Wireshark, it is important to capture traffic on the correct interfaces and ensure that SCTP decoding is enabled in the protocol preferences.

Developers writing SCTP applications on Linux will typically use the C programming language and interact with the SCTP stack through standard POSIX socket functions, extended with SCTP-specific options. The SCTP API provides access to advanced features such as stream identifiers, unordered delivery, and partial reliability. Programs must include the netinet/sctp.h header and link against the lksctp library by using the -lsctp flag during compilation. Common functions such as socket, bind, connect, listen, accept, sendmsg, and recvmsg are all extended with SCTP semantics, providing granular control over message transmission and reception.

Testing and debugging SCTP applications in Linux is facilitated by several utilities and kernel features. The /proc/sys/net/sctp directory contains tunable parameters that influence the behavior of the protocol, such as heartbeat intervals, retransmission limits, and association timeouts. Developers and system administrators can adjust these values on the fly to test different configurations or optimize performance for specific workloads. Kernel logging can also be configured to capture SCTP-related events, which can be invaluable for identifying issues during association setup, path failover, or stream management.

In distributed systems or clustered environments, SCTP offers significant benefits over TCP and UDP, and Linux is a preferred platform for such deployments due to its performance, flexibility, and configurability. Applications such as telecommunications signaling platforms, SCADA systems, and high-reliability messaging services often use SCTP to ensure uninterrupted operation even when individual network paths fail. By leveraging Linux's multi-interface capabilities and SCTP's automatic failover, these systems can deliver high availability with minimal manual intervention.

Support for SCTP is also present in higher-level frameworks and languages through bindings and libraries. For example, Python provides SCTP bindings through third-party modules that wrap the LKSCTP library. Java developers can use libraries such as the OpenJDK SCTP channel, which integrates with the NIO package. These bindings extend SCTP's reach beyond systems programming and into web services, messaging frameworks, and other application domains, all within the Linux ecosystem.

Using SCTP in Linux environments offers a robust foundation for building modern, fault-tolerant, and high-performance network applications. The protocol's integration into the Linux kernel ensures low latency and direct access to advanced features, while the rich set of user-space tools and libraries provides developers with everything needed to implement, test, and maintain SCTP-based systems. With careful configuration and a solid understanding of Linux networking, SCTP can be fully leveraged to meet the demanding requirements of contemporary communication systems.

SCTP in Windows-Based Systems

The implementation and use of the Stream Control Transmission Protocol in Windows-based systems has historically been less comprehensive compared to its integration in Linux environments, but recent developments and community contributions have made it increasingly feasible to deploy SCTP-based applications on the Windows platform. While Windows operating systems have traditionally favored TCP and UDP as primary transport protocols, the growing demand for multipath and multistream capabilities in communication systems has led to efforts aimed at bridging this gap. Using SCTP on Windows involves leveraging third-party libraries, configuring drivers, and adapting socket-based programming techniques to accommodate SCTP's advanced transport model.

Out of the box, Windows operating systems do not include native support for SCTP in the same manner that Linux kernels do. This means developers must rely on additional components to enable SCTP functionality. One of the most well-known projects that enables SCTP support in Windows is the SCTP library provided by the LKSCTP project, which has been ported to work with the Windows Sockets API through a layer of abstraction. Another alternative is the use of user-space SCTP stacks such as the usrsctp library, which is a portable SCTP implementation developed by the Internet Engineering Task Force and maintained by various contributors, including individuals from the FreeBSD and WebRTC communities.

Usrsctp is especially relevant in the context of Windows systems because it does not require kernel-level support. Instead, it operates entirely in user space, which allows it to run on systems where kernel modules cannot be installed or where administrative privileges are limited. Usrsctp provides an API similar to the Berkeley sockets interface and supports a wide range of SCTP features, including multistreaming, multihoming, partial reliability, and advanced congestion control. It has been successfully used in various cross-platform applications and is notably integrated into WebRTC for data channel communication.

To use SCTP in Windows through usrsctp, developers first include the library in their application, either by compiling it from source or linking to precompiled binaries. The API provided by usrsctp closely resembles traditional socket APIs but requires initialization and teardown procedures specific to the library. Before creating any sockets, the usrsctp library must be initialized, which involves defining a callback function that receives incoming data. After initialization, standard socket functions such as socket, bind, listen, connect, send, and receive can be used, but they must be called through the usrsctp wrapper functions. This model allows the application to operate with SCTP semantics while remaining portable across platforms, including Windows.

Windows developers who prefer native integration with Winsock can also explore projects such as the SctpDrv driver, which was developed to introduce SCTP support to Windows through a kernel-mode network driver. Although this driver is less commonly used today, it remains a valid option for those who need tighter integration with Windows networking and require SCTP support for legacy applications or proprietary systems. Installing and configuring such a driver requires administrative access and familiarity with Windows Driver Kit tools. Once installed, the driver registers SCTP as a protocol within the Windows networking stack, allowing applications to create SCTP sockets using standard Winsock calls with the appropriate protocol identifier.

When building applications that use SCTP on Windows, one challenge developers face is the limited support for SCTP in standard Windows development environments and APIs. Unlike TCP and UDP, SCTP is not recognized by default in many Windows networking tools, diagnostic utilities, and firewalls. This requires developers to configure these tools explicitly to handle SCTP traffic. Firewalls, including the built-in Windows Defender Firewall, must be configured to allow SCTP traffic on specific ports. Because SCTP uses its own protocol number (132), rules must be crafted with protocol-awareness, often requiring custom firewall configuration or third-party management tools that provide granular control over network protocols.

Network monitoring and debugging tools also vary in their level of SCTP support on Windows. Wireshark, one of the most widely used network analyzers, supports full dissection of SCTP traffic and runs effectively on Windows. It allows developers to view SCTP associations, chunk types, retransmissions, and path failover behavior in detail. Using Wireshark, developers can validate the behavior of SCTP associations and ensure that control and data chunks are correctly exchanged between endpoints. Because Wireshark operates independently of the underlying transport stack, it remains a reliable tool regardless of whether SCTP is implemented in kernel space or user space.

The performance of SCTP on Windows-based systems largely depends on the implementation used and the nature of the application. Kernel-level implementations tend to offer better performance due to reduced context switching and direct access to system resources. However, user-space implementations like usrsctp provide greater portability and flexibility, especially for applications that must operate across different operating systems with minimal changes. In performance-sensitive environments, developers may need to optimize buffer sizes, thread management, and socket handling to ensure that SCTP's advanced features do not introduce latency or overhead that affects application responsiveness.

Interoperability is another important factor to consider when using SCTP on Windows. Applications that communicate with SCTP endpoints running on other operating systems, particularly Linux, must adhere strictly to protocol standards to ensure compatibility. This includes correct handling of chunk headers, adherence to handshake procedures, and implementation of optional features such as authentication, stream reset, and error reporting. Testing across multiple platforms is essential to verify that the behavior of the SCTP stack on Windows matches that of other implementations and does not introduce subtle inconsistencies that could impact reliability.

In corporate or enterprise environments, deploying SCTP-enabled applications on Windows may also involve coordination with network infrastructure and security teams. Network address translation devices, proxies, and security appliances may not recognize SCTP traffic by default and might require firmware updates or configuration changes to allow SCTP associations to be established and maintained. Administrators must evaluate the capabilities of their network equipment and ensure that SCTP is supported at every hop, particularly when leveraging SCTP's multi-homing and path failover features that depend on transparent network traversal.

Despite the additional configuration and integration steps, SCTP on Windows provides a powerful option for developers building applications that demand high availability, low latency, and reliable transport over multiple paths. Whether implemented in user space using libraries like usrsctp or through kernel-level drivers, SCTP extends the capabilities of traditional transport layers and offers a solid foundation for next-generation network communication on the Windows platform. With appropriate planning, testing, and tooling, SCTP can be successfully deployed in Windows-based systems to enable advanced communication models and support a wide range of real-time, critical, and distributed applications.

Message-Oriented Transport for Real-Time Media

The delivery of real-time media over IP networks demands a transport mechanism that can meet strict requirements for latency, reliability, sequencing, and flexibility. In this context, message orientation plays a critical role, especially as applications increasingly rely on discrete media messages that carry timing-sensitive content such as video frames, audio packets, captions, and control signals. Traditional transport protocols like TCP and UDP have served as the backbone of internet communication, but they come with limitations that hinder their suitability for real-time media under certain conditions. The Stream Control Transmission Protocol offers a compelling alternative due to its inherent message-oriented nature and advanced features designed to support the nuanced demands of real-time media transmission.

In real-time media applications, each piece of data often represents a complete and meaningful unit. An audio codec may generate frames at fixed intervals, and a video encoder might produce compressed image data as a sequence of independent frames or groups of frames. These are not arbitrary byte streams but well-defined messages that need to be processed in whole units. TCP, which treats transmitted data as a continuous stream of bytes, fails to preserve message boundaries, forcing applications to implement their own framing mechanisms on top of the transport layer. This extra complexity increases processing overhead, introduces the potential for parsing errors, and complicates timing and synchronization across different types of media streams.

SCTP addresses this limitation by being inherently message-oriented. Each message sent through an SCTP association is preserved as a distinct unit and delivered as such to the receiver. There is no ambiguity about where one message ends and the next begins, which greatly simplifies the development of media applications that need to interpret and process complete frames or samples as they arrive. For developers, this means less time handling framing logic and more reliable handling of application-level messages, which is particularly important when working under tight timing constraints and with limited buffer capacities.

Another major advantage of SCTP for real-time media is its support for multiple parallel streams within a single association. In a multimedia context, applications often need to transmit different types of content concurrently, such as audio, video, metadata, control information, and event signaling. With TCP, all of this content is funneled through one ordered stream, meaning that a delay in delivering one segment—for example, a large video frame—can block all subsequent data, even if it is unrelated and time-sensitive, like a mute or unmute command. This problem, known as head-of-line blocking, is particularly disruptive in real-time environments where any unnecessary delay negatively impacts the user experience.

SCTP's multistreaming capability allows developers to assign different types of data to separate logical streams. This ensures that if there is a delay in delivering one stream, it does not affect the others. An audio stream can continue flowing while video experiences a momentary slowdown. Control messages can be delivered immediately, regardless of the status of media streams. This separation of streams leads to reduced latency, improved synchronization between media elements, and better responsiveness for user interactions. It also enhances fault isolation, allowing applications to recover gracefully from issues in one stream without cascading failures across the entire session.

The partial reliability extension of SCTP is another feature that aligns closely with the needs of real-time media. In many real-time applications, especially those involving live audio or video, delivering outdated data serves no purpose and may even degrade performance if it causes processing delays. SCTP supports partial reliability through the PR-SCTP extension, which allows applications to specify expiration conditions for individual messages. If a message cannot be delivered within a certain timeframe or number of retransmissions, it is discarded. This capability ensures that the transport layer does not waste resources attempting to deliver data that the application no longer considers useful, thereby preserving bandwidth and reducing queuing delays.

Congestion and flow control in SCTP are also designed to support high-quality media transmission. The protocol dynamically adjusts its sending rate based on network feedback, reducing the likelihood of buffer overflows and network saturation. While TCP implements similar mechanisms, SCTP offers more nuanced control through per-path congestion windows in multi-homed configurations, which can be particularly useful in environments where different paths have different performance characteristics. Media applications can benefit from this by routing traffic through the most reliable and lowest-latency paths, maintaining consistent delivery even when network conditions fluctuate.

Heartbeat mechanisms in SCTP play a supporting role in media delivery by enabling path monitoring and failover in multi-homed setups. When one path becomes unavailable, SCTP can reroute traffic to another path without interrupting the session. This ensures continuity for real-time sessions that must remain uninterrupted, such as teleconferences or live broadcasts. The ability to maintain association state across multiple IP addresses also opens the door for mobility scenarios, where devices move between networks but need to maintain their sessions seamlessly.

Security is another factor that cannot be overlooked in real-time media applications. SCTP includes built-in support for message authentication, which helps protect against spoofing and tampering. Media streams often contain sensitive content, whether they are part of a private video conference or a surveillance system, and it is essential that the transport protocol ensures integrity and authenticity. SCTP's optional authentication mechanisms are integrated into the protocol structure and can be applied selectively to data and control chunks, providing both flexibility and robust protection.

Debugging and monitoring of media applications over SCTP is also aided by the protocol's explicit message structure and transparent control signaling. Developers and operators can use tools like Wireshark to observe the exchange of INIT, DATA, SACK, and HEARTBEAT chunks, making it easier to identify performance bottlenecks, detect dropped or expired messages, and confirm that stream prioritization is functioning correctly. The visibility provided by SCTP at the transport level helps media engineers optimize delivery and tune system behavior in ways that are not as easily accomplished with traditional protocols.

The adaptability of SCTP to both unicast and multicast scenarios further enhances its value for real-time media. While native multicast support in SCTP is still limited, the protocol's ability to manage multiple peer associations and maintain stateful connections across varied network topologies supports many-to-one and one-to-many media scenarios effectively. This enables its use in applications like IP-based surveillance networks, collaborative virtual environments, and online broadcasting platforms, where a centralized source must reliably and efficiently deliver content to multiple receivers.

As the demand for richer media experiences continues to grow, and as devices and networks become more complex and mobile, the limitations of traditional transport protocols become increasingly evident. SCTP's message-oriented architecture provides a forward-looking solution that aligns naturally with the operational models of real-time media systems. Its ability to deliver complete messages, manage multiple parallel streams, discard stale data, and adapt to changing network conditions makes it uniquely well-suited to the requirements of modern media applications. Its transport-level innovations offer tangible benefits that simplify development, enhance performance, and ensure a higher quality of experience for users across diverse platforms and use cases.

SCTP in Telecommunication Signaling

The telecommunications industry has long demanded high levels of reliability, availability, and efficiency in signaling transport, especially as networks evolve to support increasingly complex services and architectures. Stream Control Transmission Protocol emerged from this need, developed initially to support the migration of traditional telephony signaling systems from circuit-switched infrastructures to modern IP-based networks. Its foundational role in telecommunication signaling stems from its ability to offer features absent in traditional transport protocols like TCP and UDP. SCTP was specifically designed by the IETF SIGTRAN working group to facilitate the reliable and timely transport of signaling messages used in telephone networks, particularly those based on the SS7 protocol suite.

SS7, or Signaling System No. 7, is a critical component in the architecture of traditional Public Switched Telephone Networks. It is responsible for call setup, routing, billing, number translation, SMS delivery, and other core functions. As networks transitioned to IP, there arose a need to encapsulate SS7 messages over IP without sacrificing the reliability, sequencing, and message boundary preservation essential to its operation. SCTP provided a robust solution by offering reliable, message-oriented transport with features tailored for signaling systems. Its support for multi-homing, multistreaming, and enhanced congestion control allowed signaling traffic to move away from circuit-switched paradigms while maintaining carrier-grade performance.

SCTP's message-oriented model fits perfectly with the requirements of SS7 signaling, where each message must be delivered intact and interpreted individually. Unlike TCP, which handles data as a byte stream and can fragment or coalesce messages arbitrarily, SCTP ensures that message boundaries are preserved. This eliminates the need for complex reassembly mechanisms in signaling protocols and reduces the risk of misinterpretation or message corruption. For protocols such as MTP3 User Adaptation Layer (M3UA) and SCCP User Adaptation Layer (SUA), which were created to allow SS7 to function over IP, SCTP is a critical transport component. These protocols depend on SCTP's ability to transmit discrete signaling units while providing retransmission, sequencing, and integrity guarantees.

Multistreaming is particularly significant in telecommunications signaling because it enables the parallel transmission of independent signaling messages within a single association. In legacy signaling systems, head-of-line blocking could severely impact performance, especially when a single delayed or lost message halted the delivery of all subsequent messages. With SCTP, each signaling message can be assigned to a different stream, allowing simultaneous delivery and preventing one message from delaying others. This stream separation improves throughput and responsiveness, which are essential in handling thousands or even millions of signaling transactions per second across a global network.

Multi-homing is another critical capability provided by SCTP that enhances fault tolerance in telecommunication signaling. Each endpoint in an SCTP association can bind to multiple IP addresses, allowing for redundant paths between nodes. If one path becomes unavailable due to a network failure, SCTP can seamlessly reroute traffic through another available path without disrupting the signaling session. This automatic failover capability meets the high availability requirements of telecom infrastructure, where downtime can have widespread and costly effects. For example, in a Mobile Switching Center or a Home Location Register, signaling continuity is non-negotiable, and SCTP's multi-homing ensures that systems remain operational even during link failures or routing changes.

Telecommunication signaling also benefits from SCTP's four-way handshake mechanism and cookie-based validation, which protect against certain denial-of-service attacks and prevent the unnecessary consumption of system resources. In large signaling deployments, where thousands of associations may be established, this lightweight and secure method of initiating connections ensures that only legitimate association requests result in resource allocation. This is particularly important in a threat landscape where signaling infrastructure may be targeted for disruption due to its role in managing core network functions.

The use of SCTP in telecom environments extends beyond SS7 adaptation. It is also used in the IP Multimedia Subsystem, Long Term Evolution core networks, and 5G architectures. In the IP Multimedia Subsystem, for instance, signaling protocols such as Diameter, used for authentication, authorization, and accounting, can be transported over SCTP. While Diameter is also supported over TCP and TLS, SCTP provides performance advantages when partial reliability and multistreaming are beneficial. In LTE and 5G, SCTP is used for communication between eNodeBs and the Mobility Management Entity via the S1 Application Protocol, and between eNodeBs through the X2 Application Protocol. These control-plane signaling protocols rely on SCTP's ability to deliver messages efficiently, handle large volumes of signaling traffic, and recover from failures without manual intervention.

SCTP's ability to scale and adapt makes it a future-proof choice for telecom signaling. As networks grow in size and complexity, the volume of signaling traffic increases correspondingly. New services like

IoT, mobile broadband, and ultra-low latency applications place additional demands on signaling infrastructure. SCTP is equipped to handle these demands through its efficient flow and congestion control, its capacity for managing large numbers of associations, and its modular, extensible design. These properties allow SCTP to remain relevant even as the underlying technologies and services in telecom networks evolve.

From an operational standpoint, monitoring and managing SCTP-based signaling associations are facilitated by the protocol's structured chunk-based architecture. Control messages such as INIT, SACK, HEARTBEAT, and ABORT provide network engineers and administrators with visibility into the state of associations and allow for real-time analysis of connection health and performance. In large telecom networks, this level of visibility is crucial for maintaining service-level agreements and ensuring regulatory compliance.

Implementing SCTP in telecom signaling networks requires coordination between software and network engineering teams to ensure that routing policies, firewall configurations, and hardware devices are SCTP-aware. Some legacy systems and firewalls may not handle SCTP traffic correctly unless explicitly configured to support it. Therefore, network planning and testing are critical components of a successful deployment. Once properly configured, SCTP offers a robust and scalable platform for signaling transport that meets the high demands of the telecommunications industry.

The introduction of SCTP into telecommunication signaling systems marked a shift from traditional circuit-based infrastructure to flexible, packet-switched architectures capable of supporting next-generation services. Its features provide the reliability and performance necessary for core network operations, while also supporting the evolution of telecom services into the realm of IP. Whether used in traditional SS7 networks, modern LTE control planes, or future 5G signaling environments, SCTP continues to serve as a cornerstone protocol for maintaining the seamless, resilient, and high-performance operation of global telecommunication networks.

SCTP's Role in Diameter Protocols

The Diameter protocol plays a vital role in modern telecommunications networks, providing a robust framework for authentication, authorization, and accounting functions across various services. As networks evolve to support increasingly complex architectures like LTE, 5G, and IP Multimedia Subsystems, the demands placed on transport mechanisms for signaling traffic also grow in intensity. The Stream Control Transmission Protocol has emerged as a significant transport layer solution for Diameter, offering reliability, flexibility, and performance advantages that align closely with the needs of high-availability signaling infrastructures. SCTP's unique features make it well-suited for handling the characteristics of Diameter traffic in environments where message integrity, delivery guarantees, and resilience are of paramount importance.

Diameter is inherently a message-based protocol. It transmits structured units of information called Diameter messages, which are composed of Attribute-Value Pairs and are used to manage session states, user policies, charging information, and service permissions. These messages must be delivered in full and without corruption, as incomplete or fragmented delivery can lead to serious service disruptions. SCTP, by preserving message boundaries natively within its architecture, addresses this need more effectively than stream-based protocols such as TCP. With TCP, developers must implement framing logic at the application layer to reassemble complete Diameter messages from a continuous byte stream, a process that introduces complexity and risk. SCTP eliminates this issue by delivering each message as a discrete unit, ensuring that the Diameter application on the receiving end can process it directly without ambiguity.

The multistreaming capability of SCTP is another significant advantage when used as a transport for Diameter. In traditional TCP-based implementations, all messages sent over a single connection are delivered in strict order. This ordering can introduce head-of-line blocking, where the delay or loss of one message prevents subsequent messages from being processed, even if they are unrelated. In high-throughput Diameter environments, where messages of varying types and priorities are transmitted concurrently, such blocking can degrade performance and responsiveness. SCTP's multistreaming feature allows messages to be assigned to different logical streams within a single association, each with its own independent sequencing. This means that the loss or delay of one message on a particular stream does not hold up messages on other streams, allowing Diameter servers and clients to maintain higher levels of throughput and reduced latency.

Multi-homing is yet another aspect of SCTP that enhances its utility in Diameter-based deployments. In mission-critical networks, redundancy is essential to maintain service continuity. With SCTP, each endpoint in an association can be bound to multiple IP addresses, creating multiple network paths between peers. If the primary path fails due to a link outage, hardware failure, or routing issue, SCTP can seamlessly shift communication to an alternate path without interrupting the ongoing session. This level of path resilience is a fundamental requirement in telecom infrastructures, especially for core network components like the Policy and Charging Rules Function, Online Charging System, and Home Subscriber Server, all of which rely on Diameter for continuous and uninterrupted communication.

Diameter over SCTP also benefits from the security features built into the protocol. While Diameter typically operates in secure environments and is often used with IPsec or TLS, SCTP adds another layer of protection by supporting message authentication at the transport level. The use of HMAC-based authentication chunks in SCTP helps ensure that messages have not been tampered with and that they originate from legitimate sources. This protection is particularly important in environments where signaling messages control access to services, allocate billing charges, or affect user connectivity. By combining application-layer security with SCTP's transport-level integrity mechanisms, operators can achieve a more layered and robust defense against unauthorized access or signaling manipulation.

The congestion and flow control mechanisms in SCTP also align well with the operational requirements of Diameter traffic. In dense network environments, where multiple clients may send thousands of requests per second to a central Diameter server, the risk of congestion and buffer exhaustion is very real. SCTP's selective acknowledgment feature, retransmission strategies, and adaptive congestion control allow it to manage traffic effectively, minimizing retransmissions and avoiding unnecessary overload. Furthermore, its support for partial reliability extensions allows Diameter implementations to discard less-critical messages when delivery constraints are not met, preserving bandwidth for more important transactions.

In practical deployments, operators have the flexibility to run Diameter over either TCP or SCTP, as both are supported in the Diameter protocol specification. However, SCTP is increasingly favored in applications that demand high availability, reduced message latency, and efficient parallel processing. For example, in LTE networks, the S6a interface, which links the Mobility Management Entity to the Home Subscriber Server, commonly uses Diameter over SCTP. Similarly, in 5G core networks, interfaces like N28 and N12, which involve communication between Access and Mobility Functions and Unified Data Management, can benefit from the performance characteristics of SCTP when transporting Diameter messages.

The integration of SCTP with Diameter is often supported directly in the software stacks used by telecom vendors. Diameter stacks are built with awareness of SCTP's capabilities, allowing administrators to configure association parameters, stream usage, and failover behavior to match network policies and expected traffic patterns. These stacks expose APIs that abstract away the transport details, enabling application developers to focus on message logic while relying on SCTP to ensure reliable delivery and optimal path usage. Logging, diagnostics, and performance metrics related to SCTP associations are also made available, aiding operators in capacity planning, fault detection, and root cause analysis.

In terms of interoperability, SCTP ensures consistent performance across various platforms and vendors, as its specifications are well-defined and rigorously implemented. Network engineers and architects designing Diameter-based systems must ensure that firewalls, NATs, and transport devices in the network path are SCTP-aware. While SCTP is a well-established protocol, some network elements may still require specific configuration or updates to support its traffic properly. Once these elements are in place, SCTP offers a stable and highly functional platform for transporting Diameter, meeting both the technical and operational goals of telecom network operators.

As networks continue to evolve and as user demands place greater pressure on signaling systems to be fast, flexible, and resilient, SCTP's role in transporting Diameter becomes increasingly vital. By providing message preservation, multistreaming, multi-homing, integrated security, and efficient error recovery, SCTP aligns naturally with the architectural and functional demands of Diameter in both current and next-generation networks. Its ability to enhance signaling performance, reduce latency, and safeguard communication integrity ensures that Diameter over SCTP remains a preferred and future-ready solution for service providers seeking to deliver consistent and secure user experiences at scale.

Performance in Multimedia Streaming

Multimedia streaming has become one of the most bandwidth-intensive and latency-sensitive services operating over modern networks. From video conferencing and live broadcasting to streaming platforms and interactive media applications, the demand for smooth, real-time content delivery continues to grow rapidly. This rising demand has exposed the limitations of traditional transport protocols in handling the complexity and timing constraints inherent in multimedia systems. The Stream Control Transmission Protocol offers an alternative transport layer that introduces features specifically aligned with the performance needs of multimedia streaming. SCTP addresses long-standing performance bottlenecks through mechanisms that reduce latency, preserve message integrity, enable concurrent data flows, and support resilience in variable network conditions.

Multimedia content typically consists of various data types that must be delivered in a coordinated and timely manner. A video stream may include compressed video frames, synchronized audio packets, control commands, subtitles, and metadata. Each of these components may have different tolerance thresholds for delay, jitter, and packet loss. SCTP's multistreaming capability directly benefits multimedia applications by allowing these different components to be transmitted over separate logical streams within a single association. Unlike TCP, which delivers all data through a single, ordered stream and is prone to head-of-line blocking, SCTP allows messages on one stream to be delayed or retransmitted independently without affecting other streams. This separation enhances performance by preventing unrelated delays from compounding and ensures that time-sensitive data like audio continues to flow smoothly even if a video frame or metadata message is temporarily delayed or dropped.

SCTP also provides message-oriented delivery, preserving message boundaries and ensuring that each unit of multimedia data arrives intact. This is critical in scenarios where each message represents a meaningful structure, such as a complete audio sample or video frame. With TCP, applications are required to implement complex logic to reassemble byte streams into complete messages, adding processing overhead and increasing the risk of errors. SCTP simplifies this process by delivering complete messages natively, reducing latency and processing time at the receiver. This also improves synchronization between streams, which is essential for maintaining lip-sync between audio and video or ensuring that captions appear at the correct moments in a video playback.

The protocol's support for partial reliability further enhances multimedia performance, especially in live streaming and interactive applications where timely delivery often outweighs guaranteed delivery. SCTP's Partial Reliability Extension allows developers to specify conditions under which messages should be discarded if they cannot be delivered within a certain timeframe. This prevents the retransmission of stale data that is no longer useful, such as an outdated video frame or a delayed control command. In real-time communication, delivering outdated data can be more disruptive than omitting it entirely. By avoiding unnecessary retransmissions, SCTP frees up bandwidth for more relevant content and maintains the flow of media streams without introducing noticeable lag or jitter.

Another performance factor that SCTP addresses effectively is congestion management. Multimedia streaming can involve bursty traffic patterns, where periods of high data transmission alternate with quieter intervals. SCTP's congestion control algorithms, derived and improved from those used in TCP, dynamically adjust the sending rate based on network conditions. These algorithms help avoid congestion collapse and ensure fair bandwidth sharing with other flows. When used in conjunction with selective acknowledgments, SCTP minimizes the retransmission of already received data, enhancing throughput and stability even in lossy or congested environments. For multimedia applications that operate in mobile or wireless networks, this responsiveness is crucial for maintaining quality under shifting conditions.

In environments where high availability is essential, such as broadcasting live events or delivering premium content to a global audience, SCTP's multi-homing capabilities provide a significant advantage. By allowing each endpoint to bind to multiple IP addresses and maintaining multiple network paths between peers, SCTP ensures that communication can continue uninterrupted in the event of a path failure. If one path becomes congested or unavailable, the protocol can switch to another without breaking the session or requiring a reconnection. This seamless failover mechanism reduces the risk of buffering interruptions, session drops, or user frustration during critical moments in a stream.

Buffer management and flow control in SCTP also contribute to improved streaming performance. The receiver advertises its available buffer space, and the sender adjusts its transmission accordingly. This cooperative management ensures that data is sent at a rate the receiver can handle, preventing buffer overflow and the associated packet loss or playback disruption. Efficient use of buffers leads to smoother playback and allows the application to better control latency and responsiveness, especially in scenarios where feedback mechanisms are used to adapt bitrate or resolution in real-time.

In cases where SCTP is used to transport media across diverse network environments, such as in peer-to-peer applications or distributed content delivery systems, its support for dynamic address reconfiguration and mobility-aware features provides additional flexibility. Devices that move between networks, such as mobile phones switching between Wi-Fi and cellular, can maintain their SCTP associations and continue streaming without interruption. This is especially important in today's mobile-first world, where users expect consistent service regardless of their location or the network conditions.

Diagnostic and monitoring tools also play a role in performance tuning for multimedia streaming over SCTP. Because SCTP uses a structured, chunk-based protocol with explicit signaling for connection management, retransmissions, and path monitoring, developers and network administrators can gain detailed visibility into the state of media transmissions. This visibility allows for precise tuning of parameters such as heartbeat intervals, retransmission timeouts, and stream prioritization. Tools like Wireshark provide full SCTP support, enabling real-time analysis and debugging of media streams, which is invaluable during development and deployment.

Applications that have adopted SCTP for media streaming include components of WebRTC, video surveillance platforms, telemedicine systems, and broadcast distribution networks. These use cases demonstrate that SCTP is not merely an experimental alternative but a mature and reliable solution for real-world media delivery. Its strengths in message handling, stream separation, fault tolerance, and adaptive performance position it as a transport layer protocol capable of meeting the increasingly demanding expectations of modern multimedia consumers.

SCTP's architecture aligns naturally with the operational model of multimedia streaming. By focusing on timely delivery, resilience, and efficient resource usage, SCTP enables high-quality, uninterrupted media experiences across a wide variety of network conditions and device types. As multimedia continues to dominate global internet traffic, transport protocols that prioritize adaptability, integrity, and performance will remain essential. SCTP provides a powerful foundation for streaming platforms that must deliver complex, real-time media services at scale.

SCTP and Real-Time VoIP Applications

Voice over IP technology has transformed global communication by enabling voice transmission over packet-switched networks rather than traditional circuit-switched telephone lines. As VoIP services continue to grow in popularity across enterprise and consumer markets, the requirements for low latency, high reliability, and consistent quality of service become increasingly critical. The transport protocol used to carry VoIP signaling and payload data plays a central role in meeting these demands. While protocols like UDP and TCP have historically been used for different aspects of VoIP systems, the Stream Control Transmission Protocol offers a compelling alternative that addresses several key limitations found in legacy approaches. SCTP's unique characteristics make it especially well-suited for supporting both the signaling and media layers of real-time VoIP applications.

Real-time voice communication imposes strict timing constraints on the network. Delays greater than a few hundred milliseconds can cause noticeable lag, jitter introduces choppiness, and packet loss results in gaps or distorted speech. Traditional VoIP architectures commonly rely on UDP for transporting audio streams due to its low overhead and lack of retransmission mechanisms, which suits time-sensitive data that cannot tolerate retransmission delays. However, UDP provides no guarantees of delivery, ordering, or protection against congestion, requiring the application layer to implement complex logic to mitigate its deficiencies. TCP, while offering reliability and ordering, is generally avoided for media streams because of its head-of-line blocking behavior and high retransmission latency. SCTP offers a balanced solution by combining the efficiency of UDP with the reliability of TCP, while also introducing features specifically designed for real-time communication.

One of SCTP's most important contributions to VoIP applications is its multistreaming capability. In a typical VoIP session, the system must handle various data types simultaneously, including signaling messages, voice packets, DTMF tones, presence updates, and even video or screen-sharing components in more advanced deployments. Using a single TCP stream to transport all this information can lead to delays if one component suffers loss or corruption, as all subsequent data must wait for recovery due to the strict ordering guarantees. SCTP eliminates this problem by allowing each type of data to be sent over a separate logical stream within a single association. This means that a lost control message does not delay the delivery of voice packets, maintaining call quality and responsiveness.

SCTP's message-oriented transport model is another key advantage in VoIP scenarios. Signaling protocols used in VoIP systems, such as SIP or H.248, rely on the clear demarcation of messages. TCP, being a byte-stream protocol, can fragment or combine messages arbitrarily, forcing developers to implement framing mechanisms at the application layer to reconstruct complete signaling units. SCTP preserves message boundaries natively, simplifying implementation and reducing the likelihood of message misinterpretation. This is particularly useful for SIP-based systems where exact parsing of signaling messages is required to maintain call states, negotiate codecs, manage sessions, and handle authentication.

For critical infrastructure such as call servers, session border controllers, or IP PBXs, high availability is essential. Any interruption in communication can lead to dropped calls, failed registrations, or interrupted media sessions. SCTP's support for multi-homing provides built-in redundancy at the transport level. Each endpoint can register multiple IP addresses, enabling SCTP to maintain communication even if one network path becomes unavailable. In the event of a link failure, SCTP automatically reroutes traffic through an alternate path without requiring the association to be re-established. This capability greatly enhances the resilience of VoIP systems and supports seamless failover, which is especially important for emergency communication systems, contact centers, and mission-critical enterprise telephony.

Another area where SCTP supports VoIP performance is through its partial reliability extension. In a live voice conversation, the value of audio packets diminishes rapidly as time passes. A delayed packet may be of no use by the time it is retransmitted and received. PR-SCTP allows applications to specify delivery constraints for individual messages, such as a time limit or maximum number of retransmissions. This ensures that outdated packets are discarded rather than wasting bandwidth on futile retransmission. The result is a transport protocol that aligns with the temporal sensitivity of voice communication, ensuring that resources are used to deliver only useful data.

SCTP's congestion control and flow regulation mechanisms also contribute to consistent audio quality in VoIP. Voice traffic must be delivered steadily and without excessive jitter, which requires careful management of send rates and buffer usage. SCTP's built-in congestion control, which adapts dynamically based on network conditions, helps to prevent packet loss and throttling caused by congestion. The protocol's selective acknowledgment and retransmission strategies ensure that missing data is recovered efficiently without overwhelming the network. This is particularly beneficial in shared environments where multiple users or applications compete for bandwidth, such as office networks or public Wi-Fi hotspots.

In addition to carrying voice data, SCTP can also serve as a transport layer for signaling messages in VoIP systems. For example, SIP over SCTP has been specified as an alternative to SIP over TCP or UDP. Using SCTP for SIP signaling provides several advantages, including improved resilience through multi-homing, reduced signaling latency through multistreaming, and better network behavior through built-in flow control and congestion management. These benefits are further amplified in large-scale deployments such as IMS networks or carrier-grade VoIP platforms, where the volume and variety of signaling traffic demand a transport protocol capable of handling high loads with minimal delay or disruption.

SCTP also integrates smoothly with security mechanisms important in VoIP deployments. The protocol supports message authentication, ensuring that signaling and media messages are protected against tampering and unauthorized injection. When combined with network-level encryption solutions such as IPsec or application-layer protocols like TLS or SRTP, SCTP provides a secure foundation for voice communications. Given the sensitivity of voice conversations and the increasing prevalence of VoIP-based fraud and surveillance threats, having a secure and verifiable transport layer is essential.

As VoIP technologies continue to evolve, including integration with 5G networks, WebRTC, and IoT voice assistants, the need for a transport protocol that can adapt to new requirements and use cases becomes even more critical. SCTP's extensibility, its support for multiple services within a single association, and its ability to operate efficiently in both wired and wireless networks position it as a highly relevant protocol for the future of voice communication. Its ability to maintain robust performance under varying network conditions, preserve the quality of real-time media, and deliver signaling reliably makes SCTP not only a viable option but an optimal one for enhancing the performance, reliability, and scalability of real-time VoIP applications across both enterprise and carrier networks.

Security Features in SCTP

Security is a critical aspect of any modern communication protocol, especially in an era when digital infrastructures are increasingly targeted by a wide array of threats ranging from simple packet spoofing to sophisticated denial-of-service attacks. The Stream Control Transmission Protocol was designed with several built-in security mechanisms to address common vulnerabilities observed in older transport protocols like TCP and UDP. While SCTP was originally developed to support reliable signaling in telecommunication systems, its architectural foundation includes features that inherently improve its resistance to various attack vectors, offering a more secure transport layer for both signaling and data transmission.

One of the fundamental security advantages of SCTP lies in its robust association setup process. Unlike TCP's three-way handshake, which is vulnerable to SYN flooding attacks, SCTP uses a four-way handshake with a cookie mechanism. When a client initiates an association by sending an INIT chunk, the server does not immediately allocate memory or state resources. Instead, the server responds with an INIT-ACK chunk containing a cryptographically generated cookie. This cookie includes enough information for the server to validate the request later, but it does not require the server to commit any resources at this stage. Only when the client returns the cookie in a COOKIE-ECHO chunk does the server validate it and allocate the necessary resources. This design significantly reduces the possibility of denial-of-service attacks that aim to exhaust server memory by initiating numerous incomplete connections, as the server remains stateless until the cookie is returned and verified.

Another important security feature of SCTP is the use of verification tags. Every SCTP packet contains a 32-bit verification tag in its header, which must match the tag established during the handshake process. This verification tag acts as a session identifier, preventing attackers from injecting packets into an existing association without knowledge of this value. This mechanism is similar in spirit to the Initial Sequence Numbers used in TCP but provides stronger protection due to its mandatory presence in all packets and its explicit use in validating incoming traffic. The verification tag ensures that packets not belonging to the current association are discarded immediately, making SCTP more resilient to spoofing attacks.

SCTP also supports optional message authentication using the AUTH chunk. This feature enables the integrity and authenticity of SCTP messages to be verified at the transport layer. By attaching a keyed-hash message authentication code (HMAC) to chunks that require protection, SCTP ensures that the data has not been altered in transit and that it originates from a trusted source. The authentication process uses pre-shared keys or dynamically negotiated secrets to compute and verify the HMAC. This provides protection against man-in-the-middle attacks and unauthorized modification of control or data chunks. Administrators can configure which chunk types require authentication, allowing selective security policies that balance performance with protection. For example, while it may be unnecessary to authenticate every data chunk in a multimedia stream, authenticating control chunks such as INIT, SHUTDOWN, or ABORT is critical to maintain the integrity of association management.

In addition to its authentication capabilities, SCTP supports dynamic address reconfiguration through the ASCONF chunk. This feature allows an endpoint to add or remove IP addresses from an active association, which is particularly useful in mobile and multi-homed environments. While this capability introduces flexibility, it also opens the door to potential attacks if not properly secured. To mitigate these risks, SCTP requires that all ASCONF chunks be authenticated when the AUTH feature is enabled. This ensures that only authorized changes to association parameters are accepted, protecting against hijacking or redirection attacks where malicious actors attempt to alter communication paths to intercept or disrupt data.

The chunk-based architecture of SCTP further contributes to its security posture by allowing for fine-grained control over message types and flow. Each chunk in an SCTP packet is processed independently, which simplifies the task of validating input and detecting malformed or malicious messages. This modularity also makes it easier to implement secure parsing routines, reducing the risk of buffer overflows or code execution vulnerabilities that can arise from poorly handled packet structures. Protocol extensions and future security enhancements can be introduced by defining new chunk types without disrupting the core functionality of the protocol.

Because SCTP operates at the transport layer, it can be used in conjunction with other security protocols such as IPsec or Transport Layer Security to provide additional layers of encryption and confidentiality. While SCTP itself does not encrypt data, its compatibility with existing security frameworks ensures that it can be deployed in secure environments without compromise. For applications where end-to-end encryption is a requirement, SCTP associations can be encapsulated within secure tunnels, or the application layer can implement encryption independently of the transport protocol. SCTP's support for message boundaries is particularly advantageous in these contexts, as it facilitates encryption and decryption processes by preserving the structure of discrete messages.

Firewalls and intrusion detection systems can also benefit from the explicit signaling used by SCTP. Unlike TCP or UDP, where session tracking may depend on inferred state or sequence numbers, SCTP provides clear, structured messages for initiating, managing, and terminating associations. This predictability enables more accurate inspection and enforcement of security policies at the network perimeter. Firewalls that are SCTP-aware can filter traffic based on association state, stream identifiers, chunk types, and verification tags, allowing for nuanced control over traffic flows.

SCTP's ability to support multiple streams and multiple addresses within a single association also contributes to its security resilience. In a multi-stream configuration, an application can segregate different types of data and control messages across separate streams, reducing the risk of interference or unintentional data leakage. In a multi-homed setup, the redundancy provided by multiple network paths ensures that communication can continue even if one path is compromised or under attack. This fault-tolerance is not only a performance feature but also a security measure, as it limits the effectiveness of targeted attacks on single points of failure.

Because SCTP is still not as widely deployed as TCP and UDP, it benefits from a certain degree of obscurity, which can serve as a temporary defense against automated attack tools that primarily target the more common protocols. However, this is not a substitute for robust security design. The real strength of SCTP lies in its thoughtful architecture and built-in protections, which provide a more secure foundation for transport-level communication in environments where trust, integrity, and availability are essential. From telecommunication signaling and real-time voice communication to financial systems and industrial control networks, SCTP's security features offer tangible benefits that help protect infrastructure from a growing spectrum of digital threats.

Authentication and Integrity Protection

In the landscape of modern network communication, the assurance that transmitted data is genuine and untampered is as critical as the delivery itself. As cyber threats grow in sophistication, transport protocols must evolve to offer built-in mechanisms that guarantee authentication and integrity protection. The Stream Control Transmission Protocol addresses these concerns through a well-defined set of features designed to validate the origin of messages and preserve their structure against malicious or accidental modification. By integrating authentication and integrity protection into the core protocol design, SCTP offers a more secure alternative to traditional transport protocols like TCP and UDP, which rely heavily on external layers to provide similar guarantees.

Authentication in SCTP is accomplished through the use of the AUTH chunk, a feature introduced specifically to enable verification of the legitimacy of messages between endpoints. When the AUTH mechanism is enabled, it allows the sender to attach a cryptographic signature to each chunk or selected types of chunks in a message. This signature is based on a keyed-hash message authentication code, or HMAC, computed using a shared secret known to both parties. Upon receiving the message, the recipient recalculates the HMAC using its copy of the key and compares it to the one included in the AUTH chunk. If the values match, the message is accepted as authentic. If not, it is silently discarded to prevent potential spoofing or tampering from unauthorized sources.

This model is particularly effective in protecting control messages such as INIT, INIT-ACK, SHUTDOWN, ABORT, and ASCONF. These messages are crucial to the management of SCTP associations and can significantly impact session state and path configuration. A forged or altered control chunk could allow an attacker to terminate a connection, redirect traffic, or alter routing paths. By requiring authentication for such messages, SCTP mitigates the risk of session hijacking and malicious manipulation of association parameters. The ability to define which chunk types require authentication gives system administrators and developers the flexibility to balance performance with security based on the criticality of the data being transmitted.

SCTP's authentication framework supports multiple security associations, each defined by a unique shared key identifier. This feature enables key rotation and the simultaneous use of multiple authentication policies within a single SCTP implementation. During the initial association handshake, both endpoints agree on which keys to use and what chunks must be authenticated. This negotiation ensures mutual understanding of the security parameters and allows for seamless adaptation to different levels of trust or sensitivity. The management of keys and security associations can be handled through manual configuration or integrated into broader security frameworks depending on the system's architecture and administrative policies.

Integrity protection in SCTP extends beyond simple authentication. It ensures that the data received is identical to the data sent, without alteration, whether through intentional interference or accidental corruption. SCTP provides integrity checking at multiple levels. First, every SCTP packet includes a CRC32c checksum in its common header. This checksum is computed over the entire packet, including the header and all chunks, and is verified upon reception. Unlike the simple 16-bit checksums used in TCP and UDP, CRC32c offers a much higher probability of detecting errors, making it a more robust solution for modern networks where packet corruption can occur due to hardware faults, signal interference, or buffer overflows.

While CRC32c protects against accidental data corruption, it is not a defense against deliberate modification. This is where HMAC-based authentication plays a complementary role. CRC ensures that the packet has not been unintentionally changed, and the AUTH chunk ensures that it was not maliciously forged or altered. Together, these mechanisms provide a layered defense model that is more effective than relying on any single technique. They also enable secure communication even over untrusted networks, where the threat of packet injection or alteration is real.

A notable advantage of SCTP's authentication and integrity model is its integration into the protocol's chunk-based architecture. Because each chunk in an SCTP packet can be independently verified, the protocol avoids the need for session-wide encryption or constant re-authentication of the entire stream. This granularity enables more efficient security enforcement and reduces computational overhead, particularly in systems with constrained resources or high throughput requirements. It also simplifies the processing logic for both senders and receivers, who can treat each message as an independently authenticated unit.

In multi-homed configurations, where an endpoint may be reachable via several IP addresses, authentication and integrity become even more critical. Without proper validation, an attacker could exploit path diversity to inject forged messages from an unexpected address or replay old packets across alternate paths. SCTP ensures that all packets, regardless of the interface or IP path used, are subject to the same rigorous authentication checks. The use of verification tags, in combination with the AUTH chunk, guarantees that only packets belonging to an established and validated association are processed, preventing unauthorized access or misuse of the multi-homing feature.

Deploying SCTP with authentication and integrity protection requires careful planning in terms of key management, performance tuning, and compatibility with firewalls and middleware. Some legacy network devices may not fully support SCTP or its security extensions, requiring updates or special configurations. Additionally, while SCTP can be used in conjunction with other protocols such as IPsec or TLS to provide encryption, its built-in features offer sufficient protection for many use cases where confidentiality is not a primary concern. For applications requiring both integrity and privacy, layering SCTP over IPsec is a practical approach, leveraging SCTP's message orientation and multi-streaming alongside IPsec's encryption capabilities.

Real-world applications that benefit from SCTP's authentication and integrity features include telecommunications signaling systems, where protocols like M3UA and Diameter depend on SCTP for transporting sensitive control information. In these environments, the manipulation of messages could lead to unauthorized call routing, billing errors, or service disruption. Ensuring the authenticity and integrity of messages protects the stability and trustworthiness of these critical systems. Similarly, industrial control networks, financial trading platforms, and distributed sensor infrastructures increasingly rely on SCTP to ensure that commands and data transmissions are both reliable and secure.

By embedding authentication and integrity protection into its core design, SCTP provides a comprehensive and efficient solution for securing transport-layer communication. These capabilities help to ensure that messages are genuine, unaltered, and from a trusted source, offering peace of mind in environments where even minor data corruption or unauthorized access could lead to significant consequences. SCTP's security features reflect a modern approach to protocol design, recognizing that trust and reliability must be built-in, not bolted on, and that robust communication begins with verifiable authenticity at the very first byte.

Protecting SCTP Against Flood Attacks

Flood attacks represent one of the most common and damaging threats to modern network protocols. These attacks aim to overwhelm a system by sending a large volume of requests or data, consuming computational, memory, and bandwidth resources to the point where legitimate traffic can no longer be processed. The Stream Control Transmission Protocol was specifically designed with mechanisms to address and resist such threats more effectively than older transport layer protocols like TCP. SCTP includes security-focused features that allow it to handle a wide range of flood-based attacks, particularly those targeting the association setup process, state exhaustion, and bandwidth saturation. These capabilities are embedded in the protocol architecture, providing a resilient framework for mitigating denial-of-service scenarios from the ground up.

One of the most well-known and basic forms of a flood attack is the SYN flood in TCP. This attack exploits the fact that in TCP, a server allocates resources as soon as it receives an initial SYN request, even before the client completes the handshake. Attackers take advantage of this by sending a high number of SYN packets without completing the connection, causing the server to hold these half-open connections in memory until they timeout. As the number of pending connections grows, the server's ability to accept new, legitimate requests diminishes or stops entirely. SCTP directly addresses this vulnerability with a more robust four-way handshake that uses a cookie mechanism, which delays state creation until the initiating client proves its legitimacy.

In SCTP's four-step handshake, when a client sends an INIT chunk to begin an association, the server does not immediately allocate session resources. Instead, it replies with an INIT-ACK that includes a stateless cookie. This cookie contains all the information necessary to reconstruct the server's state if the client responds, but until then, the server remains stateless. The client must return the cookie in a COOKIE-ECHO chunk, which the server verifies. Only after successful validation does the server allocate memory and finalize the association. This design prevents attackers from overwhelming the server with bogus connection requests, as no significant server resources are consumed until the attacker demonstrates the ability to receive and respond to the cookie correctly. This mechanism is especially effective against IP address spoofing, a technique commonly used in flood attacks to hide the attacker's identity and bypass basic filtering mechanisms.

Another important line of defense SCTP offers against flood attacks is its use of verification tags in all packet headers. Each association is assigned a unique verification tag during setup, and only packets containing the correct tag are processed. Packets with invalid tags are silently discarded without acknowledgment or further processing. This verification system makes it far more difficult for attackers to inject unauthorized packets into an established association or impersonate an existing session. It also reduces the risk of bandwidth amplification, a tactic in which attackers spoof requests to generate large responses from the victim, overloading their network.

SCTP also protects against resource exhaustion caused by excessive data chunk transmission. In scenarios where an attacker sends a flood of SCTP packets containing DATA chunks, the receiving endpoint must decide how to process them without compromising system performance. SCTP's flow control and congestion control mechanisms naturally mitigate this by restricting how much unacknowledged data can be in flight. The receiver advertises a window size that reflects how much buffer space is available, and the sender must respect this window. Even if the sender is malicious, the protocol restricts its ability to fill receiver buffers beyond acceptable limits. If an attacker tries to exceed these thresholds, their traffic is discarded or ignored, protecting the receiver from overload.

Authentication through the AUTH chunk further enhances protection against floods. By requiring that sensitive or critical chunks be authenticated using a pre-shared key or negotiated secret, SCTP ensures that only valid, authorized packets are processed. Malicious or spoofed chunks lacking proper authentication are rejected outright. This allows systems to filter out flood attempts that attempt to abuse features such as ASCONF, SHUTDOWN, or ABORT, which could otherwise be used to disrupt or hijack associations. Administrators can configure which chunks require authentication and tailor these settings to meet the specific threat profile of their environment.

In addition to these protocol-level features, SCTP supports rate-limiting and threshold monitoring mechanisms that can be implemented at the operating system or firewall level. For instance, an SCTP-aware firewall can monitor the rate of incoming INIT chunks and enforce a maximum rate per source IP address. If a particular source exceeds this limit, further INITs can be dropped or delayed, preventing that source from monopolizing system resources. Similar protections can be applied to COOKIE-ECHO and other control chunks, providing a layered approach to flood mitigation. These capabilities can be combined with logging and alerting systems that notify administrators of abnormal traffic patterns indicative of an active attack.

SCTP's chunk-based architecture also facilitates inspection and filtering by network security appliances. Unlike TCP or UDP, where arbitrary payload data is encapsulated in a continuous stream or datagram, SCTP defines distinct chunk types for different protocol functions. This structure allows firewalls and intrusion prevention systems to analyze and act upon SCTP traffic with more precision. For example, a system might allow only authenticated COOKIE-ECHO chunks from known IP ranges or block all ABORT chunks originating from outside a trusted network segment. This granularity makes it easier to build intelligent filters that reduce the effectiveness of flooding attempts without impacting legitimate traffic.

Multi-homing, another core SCTP feature, offers inherent protection against certain types of flooding and resource depletion. By maintaining associations across multiple IP addresses, SCTP allows data to be rerouted if one path becomes the target of a flood attack. For example, if an attacker floods one of the paths used by an SCTP association, the protocol can switch to an alternate path, maintaining communication without interruption. This redundancy not only improves availability but also distributes the attack's impact, making it harder for attackers to disrupt services entirely.

Implementation best practices also play a vital role in protecting against flood attacks. Developers should ensure that their SCTP stack adheres strictly to protocol specifications, especially in how it handles cookie validation, buffer allocation, and timeout management. Operating system vendors that implement SCTP must offer configurable parameters for controlling handshake timeouts, maximum association limits, and chunk processing rates. These parameters allow administrators to tune SCTP's behavior in response to real-world traffic loads and security requirements, enhancing resilience without compromising performance.

SCTP stands out among transport protocols for its comprehensive and integrated approach to flood attack prevention. Through a combination of stateless initiation, message verification, selective authentication, and structured message handling, SCTP mitigates many of the vectors traditionally exploited in denial-of-service and resource exhaustion attacks. These design choices reflect a modern understanding of security threats and position SCTP as a robust solution for environments where availability, trust, and reliability are non-negotiable. By embedding defenses into the core protocol design rather than relying solely on external protections, SCTP delivers a transport foundation capable of withstanding the challenges of today's adversarial internet.

NAT Traversal and SCTP Adaptations

Network Address Translation has become a cornerstone of internet connectivity, enabling multiple devices within a private network to share a single public IP address. While NAT serves critical roles in conserving address space and adding a layer of obfuscation for security, it introduces significant complications for transport protocols not originally designed with NAT in mind. TCP and UDP have undergone years of evolution to handle NAT traversal through techniques such as hole punching, port forwarding, and STUN/TURN servers. The Stream Control Transmission Protocol, with its more complex structure and enhanced capabilities, presents unique challenges when interacting with NAT devices. Nevertheless, adaptations and emerging solutions are allowing SCTP to become increasingly viable in NAT-bound environments.

At its core, SCTP was developed to address limitations in TCP and UDP, offering benefits such as multi-homing, multistreaming, and message-oriented communication. However, many of these features conflict directly with the assumptions made by traditional NAT devices. For instance, NAT systems often bind internal connections to external IP addresses and ports by tracking state information based on a tuple of source and destination IPs and ports, typically assuming the protocol is TCP or UDP. SCTP uses its own IP protocol number (132), which is not as universally recognized or handled by NAT hardware and software, especially in legacy devices. As a result, standard NATs may fail to track SCTP sessions properly, leading to dropped packets, broken associations, and unpredictable behavior.

One of the primary difficulties arises from SCTP's support for multi-homing. An SCTP association can span multiple IP addresses per endpoint, which allows for redundancy and failover. However, this poses a problem for NAT devices that typically expect a one-to-one mapping of internal and external addresses. When an SCTP endpoint initiates communication from one internal IP address and then begins sending packets from a different IP due to path failover, the NAT device may not recognize the alternate path as part of the existing session. Consequently, it may block or mishandle packets sent over these alternate routes. For multi-homing to function properly through NATs, the translation devices must be SCTP-aware and capable of recognizing all IP addresses associated with a single SCTP association—a requirement that is rarely met in consumer-grade equipment.

SCTP's four-way handshake and cookie mechanism, while enhancing security and mitigating SYN flooding attacks, also complicate NAT traversal. NAT devices typically monitor the initial handshake to determine how to establish mapping entries. In SCTP, since the server remains stateless until the COOKIE-ECHO is received and verified, the intermediate NAT may not recognize this exchange as a legitimate session setup. Additionally, NAT devices often implement short timeout periods for idle sessions. If no traffic is detected within a brief interval, the NAT will drop the mapping, breaking the SCTP association. This is particularly problematic for SCTP because it maintains persistent, long-lived associations and may go extended periods without transmitting user data.

To mitigate some of these issues, SCTP implementations often use heartbeat chunks to keep NAT mappings alive. Heartbeat messages are sent periodically to probe the health of a path and maintain session awareness on both ends. When passed through a NAT, these heartbeats can also serve as keep-alive signals, preventing the NAT from closing the session prematurely. However, the effectiveness of this approach depends on the NAT recognizing and properly forwarding these heartbeat packets, which again depends on whether it understands the SCTP protocol. In cases where it does not, heartbeats may be dropped, and the session will still be lost unless additional measures are taken.

Recognizing these challenges, the IETF has developed adaptations to help SCTP function across NAT devices. One significant advancement is the specification of SCTP encapsulation over UDP. This adaptation, known as UDP encapsulation for SCTP, allows SCTP packets to be transmitted over standard UDP ports. Since NAT devices are generally well-equipped to handle UDP traffic, encapsulating SCTP in UDP effectively disguises it as NAT-friendly communication. This method enables SCTP endpoints to traverse NAT and firewall barriers using existing infrastructure designed for UDP. The encapsulation is handled transparently by the SCTP stack, meaning that from the application's perspective, SCTP functions as usual. At the network layer, however, packets are wrapped in a UDP header, allowing them to pass through otherwise restrictive NATs.

Another approach that complements UDP encapsulation is the use of ICE, or Interactive Connectivity Establishment. Originally developed for use in WebRTC and VoIP, ICE coordinates the discovery and selection of the most efficient path between two endpoints, including those behind NATs. SCTP can be integrated with ICE by running as a transport option over UDP within ICE sessions. This combination allows SCTP-based applications to benefit from advanced NAT traversal techniques without modifying the underlying transport protocol. In this architecture, the ICE framework negotiates NAT mappings and candidates, while SCTP continues to provide its rich feature set on top of the established connection.

SCTP over DTLS over UDP is yet another layered solution designed to address both NAT traversal and security. By placing SCTP above DTLS, which itself runs over UDP, applications can achieve both secure and NAT-compatible communication. This stack is especially useful in WebRTC and similar real-time media applications where data channels use SCTP to enable reliable, unordered message transmission. DTLS provides encryption, integrity, and authentication, while UDP allows passage through NATs and firewalls. The result is a robust, secure, and flexible transport solution suitable for diverse and challenging network environments.

While these adaptations make SCTP more usable across NATs, full support still requires awareness and configuration from the infrastructure side. Firewalls and NAT devices must be configured to permit the required UDP ports and to allow long-lived associations. Additionally, endpoints should implement logic to detect failed NAT bindings and re-establish sessions when necessary. Some SCTP stacks offer APIs for monitoring NAT behavior and initiating reconnections, which is especially useful in mobile and roaming scenarios where network paths can change rapidly.

NAT traversal remains one of the key obstacles to the widespread adoption of SCTP in public internet applications. However, ongoing work in protocol encapsulation, middleware adaptation, and operating system support continues to improve its feasibility. As more systems adopt SCTP for its advanced capabilities, pressure will grow for networking equipment to evolve and support it natively. In the meantime, SCTP over UDP, integrated with ICE and DTLS, represents a practical and effective path forward. By adapting SCTP to work in NAT-bound environments without sacrificing its core strengths, developers and network architects can unlock its potential for reliable, secure, and efficient communication across the increasingly complex topologies of the modern internet.

SCTP Over IPv6 Networks

The deployment of IPv6 has introduced new possibilities and challenges for transport protocols, reshaping the landscape of network communication with a vastly expanded address space, simplified header formats, and integrated features for mobility and security. The Stream Control Transmission Protocol, with its advanced transport features, is inherently compatible with IPv6 and stands to benefit from its capabilities in ways that can improve performance, resilience, and scalability. Running SCTP over IPv6 networks enhances its potential as a robust alternative to legacy protocols such as TCP and UDP, particularly in environments that demand high availability, message orientation, and support for multihoming.

IPv6 was designed to overcome the limitations of IPv4, particularly the exhaustion of address space and the complexity introduced by NAT. With 128-bit addressing, IPv6 provides virtually limitless unique IP addresses, enabling end-to-end connectivity and reducing reliance on address translation mechanisms that often interfere with protocol behavior. For SCTP, this means that associations can be more easily formed across networks without the need for complex NAT traversal strategies. Each endpoint can advertise multiple native IPv6 addresses, aligning perfectly with SCTP's multihoming feature. The protocol's ability to bind multiple IP addresses to a single association is further empowered by IPv6, which allows for efficient path selection, failover, and load distribution across interfaces or network segments.

One of the most prominent benefits of SCTP over IPv6 is the simplification of network configuration and routing. With IPv6's stateless address autoconfiguration, devices can generate their own addresses based on network prefixes and interface identifiers, reducing administrative overhead and enabling seamless mobility. This capability complements SCTP's support for dynamic address reconfiguration. During an active association, an SCTP endpoint can use Address Configuration Change (ASCONF) chunks to inform its peer about newly available addresses or remove obsolete ones. This is particularly useful in mobile or multi-access environments, where a device may move between networks or switch interfaces. In such cases, SCTP over IPv6 allows the session to continue uninterrupted while adapting to the updated network topology.

SCTP also benefits from the clean separation of headers and payloads in the IPv6 architecture. The streamlined header design of IPv6 reduces the processing overhead on intermediate routers and simplifies the handling of extension headers. SCTP packets carried within IPv6 are identified by the next-header field set to 132, allowing firewalls and routers to recognize and process SCTP traffic explicitly. This compatibility ensures that SCTP can be integrated into modern IPv6-based infrastructure without requiring translation layers or protocol gateways. For developers and administrators, this means fewer points of failure and a more straightforward path to deployment.

Multistreaming and multihoming, core features of SCTP, become even more powerful in the context of IPv6's vast addressability and inherent support for multiple network interfaces. In a typical IPv6 deployment, each device may possess multiple global unicast addresses, link-local addresses, and potentially unique local addresses. SCTP can leverage these addresses to establish highly resilient communication paths. If one network link fails, the protocol can seamlessly continue transmission using an alternate address without requiring a new connection or impacting ongoing data exchange. This behavior is particularly advantageous for applications that require high availability, such as telecommunication signaling, real-time control systems, and financial transaction platforms.

The security architecture of IPv6 also complements SCTP's built-in protections. IPv6 mandates support for IPsec, which can provide end-to-end encryption and authentication at the network layer. While SCTP includes mechanisms such as verification tags, cookie-based handshakes, and AUTH chunks to prevent spoofing and ensure message integrity, combining SCTP with IPv6 and IPsec creates a layered security model that protects both the transport session and the data it carries. In environments where confidentiality and integrity are critical, this combination enables secure communication without relying on application-layer encryption, reducing complexity and performance overhead.

In addition to improved security and resilience, SCTP over IPv6 introduces efficiencies in mobility management. As mobile devices move across different networks, they may be assigned new IP addresses. SCTP's support for dynamic reconfiguration allows it to adapt to these changes without interrupting the association. When coupled with Mobile IPv6 or its derivatives, SCTP can maintain persistent sessions even as the underlying IP address of a device changes, facilitating uninterrupted communication for mobile clients. This capability is highly relevant for emerging applications such as connected vehicles, wearable devices, and industrial automation systems, which require constant communication even as they move between network zones.

Another area where SCTP and IPv6 intersect effectively is in support for next-generation internet services. As the Internet of Things expands and services demand more reliable machine-to-machine communication, the limitations of traditional transport protocols become more evident. SCTP's structured, chunk-based architecture and support for out-of-order delivery, partial reliability, and message boundary preservation provide a more suitable foundation for these applications. With IPv6's address richness and autoconfiguration capabilities, devices can connect and communicate more easily, while SCTP ensures that their interactions are reliable and efficiently managed.

The transition from IPv4 to IPv6 is still ongoing in many parts of the world, and dual-stack deployments remain common. SCTP implementations must therefore support both protocols and enable smooth operation across mixed environments. Most modern SCTP stacks provide dual-stack capabilities, allowing an association to be established over IPv4 or IPv6 based on network conditions or application preferences. This flexibility ensures backward compatibility while enabling forward-looking architectures that embrace the advantages of IPv6. In practice, this means that an SCTP endpoint can attempt an association over IPv6 and fall back to IPv4 if necessary, or maintain separate paths over both protocols simultaneously in a multi-homed configuration.

From a deployment standpoint, using SCTP over IPv6 requires coordination with network infrastructure, including routers, switches, firewalls, and monitoring tools. Administrators must ensure that these components recognize SCTP as a transport protocol and that IPv6 policies permit SCTP traffic. In some cases, updates to firewall rules or router configurations may be necessary to support the proper forwarding and inspection of SCTP over IPv6 packets. Network performance monitoring tools should also be configured to interpret SCTP statistics and provide visibility into traffic behavior, path health, and association status, all of which are critical for managing high-performance networks.

The deployment of SCTP over IPv6 networks represents a convergence of two powerful protocol innovations. IPv6 resolves many of the addressing and configuration limitations of IPv4, while SCTP introduces a more advanced and flexible transport layer. Together, they provide a communication framework that is robust, secure, and future-proof. SCTP gains from IPv6's larger address space, native mobility support, and simplified routing, while IPv6 benefits from having a transport layer that is resilient to failure, efficient under load, and adaptable to real-time demands. The result is a network stack that is well-suited to the demands of next-generation services and capable of supporting the growing diversity of devices, applications, and users across the global internet.

SCTP in 5G and Beyond

The evolution of mobile communication networks from 4G LTE to 5G and the future vision of 6G has created new demands for flexible, reliable, and efficient transport protocols that can support the increased complexity of network architecture and the diversity of services expected in next-generation networks. The Stream Control Transmission Protocol has become a foundational element within the signaling and control plane architecture of 5G, offering capabilities that align precisely with the goals of ultra-reliable low-latency communication, massive machine-type communication, and enhanced mobile broadband. SCTP's role in 5G is not only functional but strategic, serving as the backbone transport for key control interfaces and enabling secure and resilient communication across disaggregated and virtualized network components.

In the 5G system architecture defined by the 3rd Generation Partnership Project, SCTP is selected as the transport protocol for several core network interfaces, including the N2 and N3 interfaces connecting the gNodeB to the Access and Mobility Management Function and User Plane Function respectively. SCTP is also used in the F1-C interface between the Central Unit and Distributed Unit in split radio access networks, as well as in other internal and inter-system signaling connections. The choice of SCTP in these interfaces is intentional, driven by its support for multihoming, multistreaming, path failover, and message boundary preservation, all of which are critical in ensuring that control plane signaling remains consistent and reliable even under dynamic and failure-prone conditions.

Multihoming in SCTP provides a significant advantage in 5G networks where network slicing and cloud-native principles result in distributed components across various physical and virtual infrastructures. By allowing a single SCTP association to be maintained over multiple IP addresses, SCTP ensures continuous availability of signaling paths even when a link or network component fails. This ability to perform seamless failover without disrupting ongoing sessions is essential for 5G applications that depend on ultra-reliable low-latency communication. As network functions move to containers and virtual machines hosted across edge and central clouds, SCTP's support for path redundancy helps maintain the reliability of signaling under fluctuating network conditions.

Multistreaming allows SCTP to carry multiple independent sequences of messages over a single association. In the context of 5G, where a single logical connection might need to handle diverse types of signaling messages such as session management, mobility events, and policy updates, multistreaming prevents head-of-line blocking and allows each stream to proceed independently. This contributes to lower latency and better resource utilization, ensuring that the delivery of critical control messages is not delayed by congestion or retransmissions in unrelated streams. In a network where latency budgets are measured in milliseconds, the impact of this capability is profound.

The message-oriented nature of SCTP aligns perfectly with the structure of 5G signaling protocols. Unlike TCP, which treats data as a continuous byte stream and requires applications to delimit messages, SCTP preserves the boundaries of each message. This feature simplifies the implementation of signaling protocols such as NGAP and F1AP, as it allows direct correlation between transport-level and application-level messages without the need for additional framing or parsing logic. This not only reduces overhead but also minimizes the potential for errors in message reassembly, which is vital in maintaining the accuracy of control plane operations.

Security is another domain where SCTP provides benefits in 5G networks. While IPsec or TLS can be applied to SCTP associations for confidentiality and further integrity assurance, the protocol itself includes mechanisms such as verification tags, cookie-based handshakes, and optional authentication chunks. These features prevent session hijacking, spoofing, and unauthorized injection of signaling messages, ensuring that only legitimate peers can establish associations and exchange control messages. Given the critical nature of signaling in allocating resources, managing mobility, and enforcing policies, any compromise in signaling integrity could lead to service degradation or even outages. SCTP's security mechanisms, when properly implemented, offer a layer of protection against such threats.

In virtualized and containerized 5G deployments, SCTP operates effectively across software-defined networks and service-based architectures. Kubernetes-based deployments of network functions, for instance, require transport protocols that are both robust and flexible. SCTP's adaptability makes it suitable for cloud-native environments where pod IPs can change and where network paths are abstracted by overlay technologies. SCTP can accommodate these conditions through dynamic address reconfiguration and persistent associations that adapt to changing endpoint addresses, ensuring that signaling continuity is maintained even as the underlying infrastructure scales or moves.

As 5G networks begin to integrate with edge computing platforms, where processing is pushed closer to the end-user to meet latency and bandwidth demands, SCTP offers a transport layer that supports this distributed architecture without compromising performance. For interfaces between edge sites and core network functions, SCTP's path management and heartbeats provide mechanisms to monitor connection health, recover quickly from failures, and ensure synchronization between components that may be hosted on different physical platforms or availability zones.

Looking beyond 5G, the transport challenges of future 6G networks will likely be even more complex. 6G aims to introduce features such as integrated AI-driven network automation, native support for XR and holographic communications, and pervasive machine-type interaction with extreme reliability and near-instantaneous responsiveness. In this context, transport protocols will need to handle massive signaling densities, ultra-fine granularity of control, and dynamic, self-reconfiguring network slices. SCTP's extensibility and its core design principles make it a strong candidate to continue as a transport layer in such future scenarios. Features like stream interleaving, which allow fragments of large messages to be interleaved with other data to minimize latency, and support for partial reliability, which allows applications to prioritize time-sensitive delivery, will become even more important as data flows become more heterogeneous.

Research efforts are also exploring how SCTP can integrate more closely with emerging transport paradigms such as QUIC and software-defined networking to provide programmable and policy-aware transport. Innovations in hybrid transport architectures might combine SCTP's multistreaming and reliability features with other protocols' encryption and congestion control capabilities to form composite layers optimized for different service classes in future mobile networks. These developments suggest that SCTP's relevance is not confined to legacy or transitional systems but extends into the heart of network evolution.

The role of SCTP in 5G and beyond is a testament to its foresightful design and ability to adapt to modern network demands. As the infrastructure supporting mobile communication continues to grow in complexity, and as expectations for reliability and performance rise, SCTP's presence in the transport layer provides an essential foundation for maintaining the integrity, efficiency, and resilience of signaling communication. Its proven utility in 5G is likely just the beginning of a broader and deeper integration into the networks that will power the digital experiences of the future.

Load Balancing with SCTP Multi-Homing

Load balancing is a fundamental component of modern networking, ensuring that traffic is efficiently distributed across multiple paths or servers to optimize resource usage, minimize latency, and prevent single points of failure. In this context, the Stream Control Transmission Protocol offers a distinct advantage over traditional transport protocols through its native support for multi-homing. Unlike TCP or UDP, which typically rely on a single IP address per endpoint and require external mechanisms to handle redundancy and load distribution, SCTP inherently supports multiple IP addresses at each end of a connection. This capability not only enhances fault tolerance but also opens the door to sophisticated load balancing strategies that can be applied directly within the transport layer.

SCTP multi-homing allows each endpoint in an association to bind to more than one IP address, forming multiple potential paths between peers. These paths are monitored using heartbeat messages to ensure they remain alive and usable. In a basic configuration, SCTP selects one of these paths as the primary and uses it for all data transmission, while

97

the others serve as backups in case the primary becomes unreachable. This provides a built-in failover mechanism that ensures the continuity of communication without requiring session re-establishment. However, beyond failover, multi-homing can be used proactively for load balancing purposes by distributing traffic across available paths in a way that optimizes performance and network resource utilization.

One of the most effective ways to use SCTP for load balancing is through concurrent multipath transmission. Although SCTP's default behavior is to send user data over a single primary path, implementations can be extended or configured to transmit data simultaneously over multiple paths. This technique, sometimes referred to as bandwidth aggregation, can significantly increase throughput by utilizing the combined capacity of all available network links. It is particularly beneficial in environments where multiple interfaces are available, such as dual-WAN setups, multihomed servers, or mobile devices with both cellular and Wi-Fi connectivity. By splitting the data flow and sending different messages or chunks across different paths, SCTP reduces congestion on individual links and makes better use of total network bandwidth.

The challenge of implementing effective load balancing with SCTP lies in the decision-making process for traffic distribution. Each path may have different characteristics in terms of bandwidth, latency, reliability, and current load. A naive approach that distributes traffic evenly across all paths without considering these metrics may result in suboptimal performance, increased retransmissions, or even degraded application behavior. To address this, SCTP implementations must include path management algorithms that evaluate real-time path metrics and make dynamic decisions about which path to use for each message or chunk. Factors such as round-trip time, packet loss rate, and available buffer space are crucial inputs to these algorithms. By continuously monitoring these metrics via heartbeat acknowledgments and SACK feedback, SCTP can adapt its transmission strategy to match the current network conditions.

Another approach to load balancing with SCTP involves using different paths for different streams. Since SCTP supports multistreaming, which allows multiple logical data streams within a single association, it is possible to assign specific streams to different paths. For instance, in a multimedia application that transmits audio, video, and control signals simultaneously, each type of traffic can be mapped to a different network interface based on its latency or reliability requirements. Audio packets, which are latency-sensitive, might be sent over a low-latency path, while less time-critical video packets could use a higher-bandwidth but more variable path. Control messages could be routed through the most stable connection to ensure reliability. This selective path usage reduces interference between traffic types and enhances the overall quality of service delivered to end users.

Load balancing with SCTP multi-homing also improves system resilience. When traffic is distributed across multiple paths, the failure of a single path does not disrupt the entire flow. Instead, only the portion of traffic that was using the failed path is affected, and SCTP's path management features quickly reroute it through an alternate address. This partial failover reduces the impact on performance and maintains application continuity with minimal disruption. Moreover, the distribution of load means that no single network link becomes a bottleneck, extending the lifespan of infrastructure and reducing the likelihood of performance degradation under heavy usage.

In data center environments, SCTP's load balancing capabilities are especially useful for inter-server communication. Servers equipped with multiple NICs connected to redundant switches can form multihomed SCTP associations with peer servers or front-end load balancers. The transport protocol itself can be tasked with distributing traffic across interfaces, reducing the need for higher-layer load balancing proxies or complex routing configurations. This model simplifies network design, lowers latency by avoiding unnecessary hops, and improves scalability by decentralizing the load balancing function.

The integration of SCTP load balancing strategies into software-defined networking and network function virtualization environments further enhances their effectiveness. In SDN architectures, network controllers can programmatically instruct SCTP endpoints on preferred path selection based on global network knowledge. This enables coordinated traffic steering across multiple flows, balancing the overall network load rather than just that of individual associations. In NFV deployments, virtualized network functions that support SCTP can migrate across data centers without breaking ongoing sessions, leveraging SCTP's ability to adapt to new IP addresses via dynamic address reconfiguration.

From a deployment perspective, using SCTP for load balancing requires careful planning and support from both the operating system and the network infrastructure. Firewalls and routers must be configured to recognize and allow SCTP traffic, including its control chunks like INIT, HEARTBEAT, and SACK. Monitoring tools should be adapted to track per-path statistics and provide visibility into traffic distribution and path performance. Where native SCTP support is limited, such as in older NAT devices or middleboxes, UDP encapsulation or tunneling solutions may be used to preserve SCTP functionality across heterogeneous network environments.

As the demand for high-availability, high-throughput, and low-latency communication continues to grow across sectors such as finance, healthcare, telecom, and cloud services, SCTP's multi-homing and load balancing features offer a powerful, protocol-level solution. Unlike external load balancing appliances or complex failover scripts, SCTP embeds intelligence directly within the transport layer, enabling applications to benefit from seamless performance optimization and robust connectivity with minimal overhead. By leveraging multi-homing not just for redundancy but for active traffic management, SCTP delivers a level of transport-layer sophistication that meets the performance and reliability expectations of modern digital services.

Reliability and Ordered Delivery Guarantees

In any communication protocol designed to support critical data exchange across networks, reliability and the preservation of message order are foundational requirements. The Stream Control Transmission Protocol was developed with the intent to meet and exceed the reliability guarantees offered by traditional transport protocols, while also resolving some of the inherent limitations associated with those protocols. Unlike TCP, which offers reliable and ordered delivery but suffers from issues like head-of-line blocking and lack of multistreaming, SCTP provides a more advanced and flexible set of tools to ensure that data is delivered accurately, in sequence where required, and with mechanisms that adapt to the nature of the application and network conditions.

At the core of SCTP's reliability model is its chunk-based transmission structure. Every data unit in SCTP is encapsulated into a data chunk, each of which is assigned a unique Transmission Sequence Number. These sequence numbers allow the receiving side to reassemble messages correctly and detect any losses or duplications. The receiver acknowledges received data using Selective Acknowledgment chunks, which provide detailed feedback about which chunks have arrived and which are missing. This selective acknowledgment approach is more efficient than TCP's cumulative acknowledgment model because it enables precise retransmission of only the missing data chunks rather than potentially unnecessary retransmissions of contiguous data. As a result, SCTP can maintain high throughput and efficiency even over lossy or congested network paths.

Reliability in SCTP also depends on its retransmission mechanisms. The protocol maintains timers for every transmitted data chunk, and if an acknowledgment is not received within the expected timeframe, the data is retransmitted. The timeout interval is dynamically adjusted based on round-trip time measurements, allowing SCTP to adapt to network conditions and avoid unnecessary retransmissions in high-latency environments. Additionally, if the receiver repeatedly signals that a specific data chunk is missing by sending multiple SACKs referencing the same gap, SCTP initiates fast retransmission of the missing chunk, bypassing the timeout period. This capability minimizes recovery time and improves responsiveness in real-time applications.

An important element of SCTP's reliability is its support for multiple simultaneous paths through multihoming. If an SCTP association is established between endpoints with multiple IP addresses, each data chunk is transmitted over the primary path, but alternate paths are available in case of failure. SCTP monitors the status of each path using heartbeat messages and dynamically reroutes traffic if the primary path becomes unresponsive. This failover mechanism ensures that ongoing data transmission continues uninterrupted even in the event of link degradation or failure. When used in critical systems such as telecommunication signaling or financial transaction networks, this feature dramatically enhances the robustness and availability of services.

SCTP guarantees ordered delivery within streams. Unlike TCP, where all data must be delivered in order and loss or delay in any segment stalls the entire stream, SCTP supports multiple independent streams within a single association. Each stream has its own sequence numbering and delivery order, ensuring that messages within a stream arrive in the correct order while not blocking data in other streams. This prevents the classic head-of-line blocking problem and allows concurrent delivery of unrelated data. Applications that transmit a mixture of control messages, media content, and status updates can assign different streams to different message types, maintaining order where necessary and avoiding unnecessary delay where order is not critical.

For applications that require strict ordering, SCTP allows developers to enforce in-sequence delivery on a per-stream basis. When a message is sent, the application specifies the stream identifier and whether ordered delivery is required. If ordered delivery is selected, SCTP holds subsequent messages in the stream until all preceding messages have been received and acknowledged. This preserves the logical sequence of operations or events, which is essential in systems like command-and-control networks or serialized data exchanges where the order of operations affects system behavior.

While reliability and ordered delivery are essential for many applications, SCTP also supports flexibility through partial reliability extensions. Some use cases, such as real-time audio or video streaming, can tolerate a certain degree of message loss if it helps reduce latency. SCTP allows applications to specify expiration parameters for individual messages. If a message cannot be delivered within a specified time window or after a certain number of retransmission attempts, it can be discarded. This feature lets developers strike a balance between strict reliability and responsiveness, optimizing protocol behavior according to the specific demands of their applications.

The protocol's support for fragmentation and reassembly also contributes to its reliability guarantees. SCTP can handle large messages by fragmenting them into multiple chunks, each of which is transmitted and acknowledged independently. At the receiving end, these fragments are reassembled into the original message once all chunks have arrived. This fragmentation process is transparent to the application, allowing large payloads to be sent without requiring manual segmentation or reassembly logic. It ensures that large data units are reliably delivered without overwhelming buffer capacities or encountering path Maximum Transmission Unit limitations.

SCTP's architectural decisions reflect a comprehensive understanding of real-world communication challenges. Its combination of per-chunk acknowledgment, selective retransmission, multi-path redundancy, and stream-based ordering represents a mature evolution of the transport layer. The protocol anticipates and addresses issues that are particularly pronounced in modern networking environments, such as dynamic routing, heterogeneous data flows, and the need for fine-grained control over reliability behavior. Applications that leverage SCTP benefit from its ability to ensure data integrity and correct sequencing even in adverse network conditions.

Reliability and ordered delivery are not abstract guarantees in SCTP but are embedded in each phase of communication—from the initiation of an association through the delivery of each individual message. The protocol ensures that no message is accepted unless it has been verified, sequenced, and, when necessary, authenticated. By offering this level of control and assurance, SCTP becomes an ideal transport solution for systems where consistency, fault tolerance, and timing precision are critical. Whether used in telecommunications, finance, military communications, or industrial control systems, SCTP's reliability and ordered delivery guarantees provide the foundation for trusted and predictable data exchange in a wide variety of mission-critical applications.

SCTP Failover Mechanisms

The ability of a transport protocol to recover quickly and efficiently from network path failures is essential in maintaining communication continuity, particularly in systems that demand high availability and reliability. The Stream Control Transmission Protocol was designed from the ground up with resilience in mind, incorporating native failover mechanisms that allow associations to remain active even when individual network paths become unreachable. Unlike TCP, which typically relies on a single source and destination IP address pair and requires external solutions or complex reconfiguration to handle path failure, SCTP introduces failover as a standard feature through its support for multihoming and dynamic path management. These capabilities enable seamless redirection of traffic, preserving both the association state and the ongoing data exchange.

SCTP's approach to failover is deeply integrated into its architecture. During association establishment, each endpoint can advertise multiple IP addresses. These addresses are maintained within the association as part of the peer's address list, and SCTP treats all of them as valid destinations for the session. Although only one path is selected as the primary path for data transmission, the others are continuously monitored through heartbeat mechanisms. Heartbeat chunks are lightweight control messages periodically sent over each alternate path to test connectivity. If a path fails to respond within a defined number of retransmissions or heartbeat attempts, it is declared inactive. This detection process is managed internally by the protocol and does not rely on intervention from the application layer.

The failover mechanism is triggered when the primary path is declared inactive. At that point, SCTP automatically selects one of the alternate paths that is still marked as active and redirects the traffic through it. This transition is transparent to the application and requires no renegotiation of the session or reestablishment of the association. By preserving the session state and sequence numbers, SCTP ensures that data transfer can continue without interruption or data loss, even if the physical or logical network topology changes unexpectedly.

Path selection during failover can be influenced by multiple factors, including the path's round-trip time, historical reliability, and configuration preferences. SCTP implementations may use a path management algorithm to rank alternate paths and determine the most suitable candidate for failover. In environments where certain paths offer better performance characteristics, administrators can configure path priorities to guide SCTP's failover decisions. This flexibility allows for failover not only as a reactive measure but also as a proactive strategy to maintain optimal performance. For instance, in a scenario where a wireless link becomes degraded due to interference, SCTP can shift traffic to a more stable wired path even before complete failure is detected.

The speed of SCTP's failover process is critical to minimizing the impact of path failures on real-time applications. Heartbeat intervals and path failure thresholds can be tuned to balance sensitivity and stability. Lowering the heartbeat interval and reducing the number of missed responses required to declare a path inactive can lead to faster failover, but may also increase the likelihood of false positives in environments with transient delays. Conversely, more conservative settings reduce the chance of premature failover but may result in longer outages when a path genuinely fails. Selecting the appropriate parameters depends on the application's tolerance for disruption and the expected network conditions.

In addition to failover for data traffic, SCTP also ensures that control and signaling messages are rerouted appropriately. This is especially important in systems where control channels must remain synchronized with data channels, such as in telecommunications signaling networks or industrial control systems. SCTP's chunk-based architecture facilitates the redirection of all types of messages, regardless of content or purpose, ensuring that the entire communication stack remains functional during and after a failover event.

SCTP failover also supports recovery from simultaneous failures. In a well-designed multihomed environment, each endpoint should be connected through independent network interfaces, routers, and service providers to maximize redundancy. SCTP can navigate complex failure scenarios where multiple paths fail at once by maintaining awareness of all advertised addresses and probing them independently. If no path is available, the protocol enters an idle state but retains the association context. Once a viable path is restored, SCTP resumes normal operation without requiring the application to reinitiate the session. This capability makes SCTP particularly valuable in systems with strict uptime requirements or in remote deployments where manual recovery is not feasible.

Integration with higher-level services also enhances SCTP's failover behavior. In cloud-native or software-defined networking environments, SCTP can interact with orchestration layers that dynamically allocate network resources and respond to failures by instantiating new paths or rerouting traffic across overlay networks. SCTP's failover mechanisms can complement these dynamic systems by maintaining session continuity while the infrastructure adapts, providing a transport layer foundation that aligns with the goals of automation and elasticity.

In mobile networks, where endpoints may change IP addresses frequently due to handovers or network transitions, SCTP failover mechanisms extend to dynamic address reconfiguration. Using the ASCONF chunk, endpoints can add or remove IP addresses from an existing association, allowing SCTP to track changes in endpoint reachability and respond accordingly. This is especially beneficial in scenarios where mobile nodes move across different networks or between wireless and wired connections. Failover in such contexts is not merely a matter of selecting a new path, but also updating the association to reflect current network realities while preserving session state and ongoing communication.

Monitoring and diagnostics tools can observe and log SCTP failover events, providing valuable insights into network health and application resilience. Metrics such as the frequency of path failures, time to recovery, and success rates of alternate paths can inform capacity planning and network optimization. In mission-critical systems, this data can be used to refine failover strategies and ensure that the most reliable paths are prioritized. The visibility provided by SCTP's internal control messages also supports proactive maintenance, as network administrators can identify degrading paths and address potential issues before they result in complete failure.

SCTP failover mechanisms are not only technically robust but also operationally transformative. By embedding failover logic directly into the transport layer, SCTP reduces the complexity of building resilient applications. Developers can focus on application logic, confident that the underlying transport will adapt to network changes without disrupting service. This separation of concerns leads to cleaner design, reduced overhead, and faster development cycles. It also enhances user experience by delivering consistent connectivity even in the face of infrastructure failures.

In a networking landscape increasingly defined by mobility, virtualization, and distributed architecture, SCTP's failover capabilities provide a critical advantage. Its proactive and reactive path management, seamless session continuity, and application transparency position it as a protocol of choice for systems where reliability cannot be compromised. Whether used in telecommunication signaling, financial transactions, industrial automation, or cloud-native microservices, SCTP delivers failover performance that aligns with the expectations of modern networked systems.

Integration with WebRTC Components

The integration of the Stream Control Transmission Protocol into WebRTC components represents a critical evolution in real-time communication technologies, enabling rich, reliable, and efficient data exchange across browsers and mobile applications. WebRTC, which stands for Web Real-Time Communication, is a set of protocols and APIs that allow audio, video, and data sharing between peers without requiring plugins or external software. From its inception, WebRTC was designed to support secure and responsive peer-to-peer communication over the open internet, and SCTP was chosen as the foundation for one of its most important subsystems—the Data Channel.

WebRTC Data Channels enable the transmission of arbitrary data between peers. This functionality is essential for applications like file transfer, multiplayer gaming, collaborative editing, messaging, and any service where user-defined data types must be exchanged reliably and efficiently. The unique characteristics of SCTP make it ideal for this role. Unlike TCP, which provides a continuous byte stream and enforces strict ordering, or UDP, which offers no guarantees, SCTP provides a flexible, message-oriented approach that supports both ordered and unordered delivery, as well as options for partial reliability. These features align closely with the demands of modern real-time applications, which often require custom transport behavior for different types of data.

In the context of WebRTC, SCTP is not used directly over IP. Instead, it is layered on top of the Datagram Transport Layer Security protocol, which itself runs over User Datagram Protocol. This encapsulation model is necessary to ensure security and NAT traversal, both of which are non-negotiable requirements for WebRTC. Because most clients operate behind NATs and firewalls, direct SCTP over IP would face significant compatibility issues. By encapsulating SCTP within DTLS and UDP, WebRTC leverages existing NAT traversal techniques, including ICE (Interactive Connectivity Establishment), STUN (Session Traversal Utilities for NAT), and TURN (Traversal Using Relays around NAT), to establish reliable connections across different networks.

The resulting stack—SCTP over DTLS over UDP—provides a secure, reliable, and flexible channel for data transport in WebRTC sessions. DTLS ensures that data is encrypted and authenticated, protecting against eavesdropping and tampering. SCTP, running over DTLS, maintains its ability to manage multiple streams, perform selective retransmissions, and offer application-specific delivery guarantees. For instance, a WebRTC-based application can establish multiple logical streams over a single SCTP association, with each stream configured for different delivery modes. A messaging stream can be set to ordered and reliable delivery, ensuring that messages arrive in sequence and without loss, while a telemetry stream might be configured for unordered and partially reliable delivery, allowing newer updates to overwrite outdated ones without the burden of retransmission.

The integration of SCTP into WebRTC also benefits from its support for congestion control and flow management. WebRTC applications must operate effectively over diverse network conditions, including mobile connections, Wi-Fi networks, and high-speed wired environments. SCTP's ability to adapt to changing network bandwidth and round-trip times ensures that data channels remain responsive and efficient. Moreover, SCTP's chunk-based framing allows for precise message sizing and management, enabling large messages to be split across multiple packets and reassembled correctly on the receiving end. This behavior is particularly useful when sending large files or streaming structured data such as JSON objects or binary formats.

Another advantage of SCTP within WebRTC is its resilience to packet loss and path changes. SCTP was designed to maintain session state even if the underlying path changes, a property that aligns well with the mobile-first nature of modern web applications. While native SCTP uses IP-layer multihoming for path failover, the WebRTC stack achieves similar resilience through the ICE framework, which can switch between network candidates if connectivity degrades. SCTP continues to operate seamlessly over the new path without application intervention, preserving the continuity of the Data Channel session.

Developers building applications with WebRTC often interact with SCTP indirectly through high-level APIs such as RTCDataChannel. These APIs abstract away the complexity of the underlying protocol stack, allowing developers to open data channels, send messages, and register event handlers for message receipt or state changes. Under the hood, however, these interactions are powered by the SCTP association managed by the WebRTC engine, typically implemented in browser-native code or supporting libraries like libwebrtc. As a result, developers gain the benefits of SCTP—such as message ordering, stream separation, and delivery control—without needing to manage the protocol's intricacies themselves.

The successful integration of SCTP into WebRTC also requires careful attention to compatibility and interoperability. Different browsers and platforms may implement varying versions or configurations of the SCTP stack, making it essential for application developers to perform thorough testing across environments. Issues such as maximum message size, stream limits, and error handling behaviors must be validated to ensure consistent application performance. In practice, most modern browsers adhere closely to the WebRTC specifications defined by the W3C and IETF, including the use of SCTP for data channels as defined in the relevant RFCs. However, developers must remain aware of evolving standards and update their applications accordingly.

Security considerations also play a significant role in the integration of SCTP with WebRTC. Since WebRTC sessions are established between untrusted peers over the public internet, all communication must be protected. DTLS provides the cryptographic foundation for this protection, while SCTP contributes to the trust model by verifying association state and ensuring message integrity. Together, these protocols form a secure pipeline that resists interception, spoofing, and tampering. For applications involving sensitive user data, compliance with privacy standards and regulatory frameworks depends on this layered security architecture.

As WebRTC continues to evolve, the role of SCTP is likely to expand. Emerging applications in areas such as augmented reality, collaborative design, and decentralized communication systems require more sophisticated transport capabilities than TCP or UDP alone can provide. SCTP's multistreaming and partial reliability features offer a compelling foundation for these scenarios. Additionally, ongoing research into improving SCTP performance over mobile and high-latency networks may yield optimizations that further enhance its value in WebRTC contexts.

The adoption of SCTP within WebRTC demonstrates the protocol's adaptability and relevance in modern communication ecosystems. By enabling efficient, reliable, and secure data transfer within browser-based applications, SCTP fulfills a critical function that would be difficult to replicate using other transport protocols. Its message-based design, support for multiple delivery modes, and integration with security and NAT traversal layers make it an essential component of WebRTC's architecture. As developers and users continue to demand more from real-time web applications, the capabilities provided by SCTP will remain central to delivering high-quality, interactive experiences across the open internet.

SCTP in Real-Time Gaming Applications

Real-time gaming applications demand an exceptional level of responsiveness, reliability, and adaptability from the underlying network infrastructure. These applications rely on continuous, low-latency data exchanges between players and game servers or between peers in multiplayer environments. Traditionally, game developers have favored UDP for real-time communication due to its minimal overhead and speed, sacrificing reliability and ordering in favor of raw performance. However, as games become more complex and as expectations for quality and stability rise, the limitations of UDP become increasingly evident. The Stream Control Transmission Protocol provides a compelling alternative by offering a unique combination of reliability, message orientation, stream separation, and support for partial reliability, making it particularly well-suited for real-time gaming applications that must balance speed with data integrity.

SCTP introduces features that directly address many of the shortcomings developers face when using either UDP or TCP for gaming. While TCP ensures reliable and ordered delivery, it enforces strict sequencing for all data, causing delays in the entire stream if any packet is lost or arrives out of order. This behavior, known as head-of-line blocking, is particularly detrimental in fast-paced games where different types of messages have different timing sensitivities. UDP avoids this problem by transmitting data without guarantees, but this can result in lost, duplicated, or out-of-sequence packets, forcing developers to implement complex reliability mechanisms in the application layer. SCTP strikes a balance between these two extremes by offering optional per-stream ordering, selective retransmission, and message boundary preservation, all within a single, integrated transport protocol.

One of the most important features that SCTP offers for gaming is multistreaming. This allows a single SCTP association to carry multiple independent logical streams of data, each with its own sequence numbers and ordering guarantees. In a multiplayer game, different types of data are sent simultaneously: player movement updates, action confirmations, game state synchronization, voice communication, and chat messages. With SCTP, each of these data types can be assigned to a separate stream, enabling the protocol to maintain independent delivery guarantees per stream. For example, voice packets and movement updates can be transmitted in an unordered, partially reliable manner to reduce latency, while chat messages and game state updates can be delivered reliably and in order to ensure correctness. This separation prevents less critical or time-sensitive messages from blocking the delivery of more important ones, resulting in smoother and more predictable gameplay.

The message-oriented nature of SCTP is another advantage in gaming scenarios. Unlike TCP, which delivers data as a continuous byte stream, SCTP treats each message as a discrete unit and ensures that message boundaries are preserved. This simplifies the processing of game events on the receiving end, as each message arrives in its complete form and can be interpreted immediately without the need to reconstruct it from a stream of bytes. This reduces the complexity of the game logic and avoids errors that can arise from incomplete or misaligned message boundaries. In fast-moving games, where timing and precision are critical, this kind of structured message delivery enhances both efficiency and accuracy.

Partial reliability, supported through SCTP's PR-SCTP extension, is especially useful in real-time gaming. Some types of data, such as periodic position updates or sensor inputs, lose their value if delayed. Resending such data after a certain point not only wastes bandwidth but can also cause gameplay inconsistencies. SCTP allows developers to specify expiration times or transmission limits for individual messages. If a message cannot be delivered within the defined window, it is dropped, making room for newer and more relevant data. This feature enables the transport layer to align with the game's logic and priorities, ensuring that the most useful data reaches its destination in time to impact the game state.

SCTP also provides enhanced resilience through multi-homing. In a gaming environment, where connectivity is essential to the user experience, even a brief disconnection can result in lost progress or player frustration. SCTP supports multiple network paths for each endpoint, allowing an active association to continue over an alternate IP address if the primary path fails. This is particularly beneficial in mobile gaming, where users may switch between Wi-Fi and cellular networks or move between access points. SCTP's ability to seamlessly detect path failures using heartbeat messages and switch to backup paths without dropping the session ensures continuity in gameplay, even during network transitions.

Security is another area where SCTP benefits gaming applications. Many games are subject to abuse through packet injection, replay attacks, or session hijacking. SCTP mitigates these threats through its verification tag mechanism, cookie-based four-way handshake, and optional message authentication via HMAC. These built-in security features protect the integrity of gaming sessions without requiring the application to implement its own transport-layer security logic. When combined with DTLS in environments such as WebRTC-based gaming or when running over UDP for NAT traversal, SCTP ensures that communication remains secure, authenticated, and resistant to tampering.

In peer-to-peer gaming scenarios, where players communicate directly rather than through a central server, SCTP works well in conjunction with NAT traversal techniques. By encapsulating SCTP over UDP, games can benefit from SCTP's advanced transport features while still leveraging ICE, STUN, and TURN to establish and maintain connections across different network topologies. This is particularly useful in casual or browser-based games that rely on WebRTC data channels, where SCTP provides the backbone for reliable messaging between clients in real time.

Despite its advantages, SCTP adoption in gaming has been relatively limited due to the dominance of TCP and UDP in game engine APIs and network libraries. However, as network conditions grow more complex and as users demand better performance and fewer interruptions, the case for SCTP becomes stronger. Game developers seeking to build robust, scalable, and responsive networked experiences should consider the capabilities that SCTP brings to the table. Its ability to offer configurable reliability, preserve message structure, support multiple streams, and recover from path failures gives it a unique edge over older protocols, particularly in the context of modern gaming environments that span mobile, desktop, and browser platforms.

SCTP's flexibility allows it to serve the diverse needs of gaming applications across genres, from first-person shooters and strategy games to racing titles and online RPGs. Whether used for server-client communication or peer-to-peer messaging, SCTP enables more control over how and when data is transmitted and received. In a landscape where milliseconds matter and user expectations continue to rise, leveraging the advanced transport features of SCTP can lead to more immersive, stable, and satisfying gaming experiences. As support for SCTP grows within engines, libraries, and platforms, its role in shaping the future of real-time gaming will become increasingly prominent.

High Availability Systems with SCTP

High availability systems are designed to maintain continuous operation and service delivery despite failures in hardware, software, or network infrastructure. These systems are essential in industries such as telecommunications, finance, transportation, and healthcare, where downtime can result in significant financial losses, safety risks, or degraded user experience. The Stream Control Transmission Protocol offers an architecture that inherently supports the principles of high availability through its built-in mechanisms for redundancy, fault tolerance, seamless failover, and robust connection management. These features enable SCTP to serve as a critical transport layer in systems where reliability, resilience, and minimal disruption are fundamental requirements.

At the heart of SCTP's contribution to high availability is its support for multihoming. Multihoming allows each endpoint in an SCTP association to maintain multiple IP addresses. Unlike TCP, which typically establishes a connection between a single pair of IP addresses, SCTP maintains an association that can span several network paths simultaneously. This allows for automatic failover if the primary path becomes unreachable due to network issues, hardware failure, or maintenance events. SCTP continuously monitors the health of each path using heartbeat messages, which probe the availability and responsiveness of alternate routes. If a heartbeat fails to receive a response within a predefined interval, SCTP marks the path as inactive and reroutes traffic through a functional path without terminating the session or requiring reestablishment.

This capability is essential in high availability systems where service continuity must be preserved even under adverse network conditions. For example, in a telecommunications environment where signaling traffic must be maintained between mobile switching centers and home location registers, the ability of SCTP to maintain persistent associations across redundant paths ensures that call setup, billing, and mobility management remain uninterrupted. Similarly, in financial systems that require constant synchronization between trading platforms and settlement servers, SCTP ensures that critical data continues to flow even during link degradation or device failure.

Another advantage of SCTP in high availability systems is its chunk-based and message-oriented design. SCTP does not treat data as a continuous stream of bytes but rather as discrete messages encapsulated in chunks. Each message maintains its integrity during transmission and is delivered as a complete unit. This simplifies the logic for high availability systems that rely on transactional integrity or command-response patterns. The protocol preserves message boundaries, ensuring that the recipient receives the message exactly as intended, which is essential for systems that depend on strict formatting or structure, such as control systems and machine-to-machine communications.

SCTP's support for multistreaming further enhances its utility in high availability deployments. Multiple logical streams can be created within a single association, each capable of independent sequencing and delivery. This prevents head-of-line blocking, a common problem in TCP, where a delayed or lost packet can halt the progress of all subsequent data regardless of its relevance or urgency. In contrast, SCTP allows unrelated streams to proceed without delay, ensuring that essential operations are not blocked by less critical ones. In a system that handles various levels of priority data, such as status updates, command signals, logging information, and real-time alerts, SCTP's multistreaming capability ensures that high-priority messages are delivered without interference.

High availability systems also benefit from SCTP's four-way handshake mechanism, which is used to establish associations securely and efficiently. This handshake, which includes the use of cryptographic cookies, ensures that resources are allocated only after the authenticity of the peer is verified. This mitigates the risk of denial-of-service attacks that exploit resource allocation during connection setup. Unlike TCP's three-way handshake, which commits resources upon receiving a SYN request, SCTP remains stateless until the final handshake step is completed. This is particularly useful in systems with limited resources or in environments where service availability must be protected against malicious or malformed traffic.

Dynamic address reconfiguration is another SCTP feature that supports high availability. Through the use of ASCONF chunks, an SCTP endpoint can add or remove IP addresses from an existing association. This means that a node can adapt to changes in network topology or interface availability without interrupting the session. For example, if a server acquires a new IP address or transitions from one network interface to another due to failover, it can notify its peers and continue communication seamlessly. This dynamic flexibility reduces the need for manual reconfiguration and minimizes downtime during network reorganization.

In virtualized and cloud-native environments, SCTP offers additional benefits for maintaining high availability. As services are deployed in containers and managed by orchestration tools like Kubernetes, network paths and endpoints can change rapidly. SCTP's resilience to address changes and its support for persistent associations make it well-suited for these dynamic infrastructures. Load balancers and ingress controllers can route SCTP traffic to backend services with confidence that the protocol will maintain session integrity, even if the physical or virtual location of a service instance changes.

Monitoring and diagnostics play an important role in sustaining high availability, and SCTP supports this through its internal state machines and detailed feedback mechanisms. Administrators can track the health of each path, monitor retransmission activity, and observe the status of associations in real time. Tools like Wireshark provide deep visibility into SCTP sessions, exposing heartbeat exchanges, chunk retransmissions, and control messages. This transparency allows operators to detect potential issues before they impact service availability and to perform root cause analysis when failures do occur.

SCTP's robustness can be further enhanced by combining it with additional technologies such as IPsec for encryption, VRRP for IP-level redundancy, and BGP for dynamic route management. These integrations create a multi-layered defense against failure, where SCTP ensures transport-level resilience while the underlying network and system layers provide complementary protection. In high availability architectures where multiple layers must work together, SCTP serves as a reliable and flexible transport layer that bridges diverse systems and ensures the uninterrupted flow of critical information.

High availability systems depend not only on the ability to resist failure but also on the capacity to recover quickly and operate without noticeable degradation. SCTP's design addresses both aspects by offering features that maintain connection stability, adapt to changing network conditions, and provide continuous service under stress. Its suitability for signaling, control, and transactional data makes it an ideal transport layer in scenarios where performance, reliability, and adaptability are non-negotiable. As digital infrastructure becomes more complex and as service expectations continue to rise, the role of SCTP in enabling high availability will continue to expand across industries and applications.

SCTP in SCADA and Industrial Systems

Supervisory Control and Data Acquisition systems are the backbone of modern industrial environments, providing centralized monitoring and control over remote equipment and processes in energy, manufacturing, water treatment, transportation, and many other sectors. These systems are responsible for collecting real-time data, issuing control commands, managing alarms, and enabling operators to respond quickly to changing conditions. The communication protocols used in SCADA systems must support high reliability, timely delivery, resilience to failure, and flexibility in network configurations. The Stream Control Transmission Protocol presents a strong candidate for the transport layer in SCADA and other industrial systems due to its unique combination of reliability, fault tolerance, multistreaming, and support for message-based communication.

Industrial environments are increasingly moving away from legacy serial communications and proprietary protocols toward IP-based architectures. In these environments, the network layer must deliver deterministic and predictable communication even over shared and sometimes unreliable networks. SCTP provides several features that make it especially suitable for these requirements. Its multihoming capability allows both SCADA master stations and remote terminal units to maintain multiple network paths for redundancy. This ensures that if a primary path becomes unavailable due to link failure, hardware outage, or maintenance, SCTP can seamlessly switch to an alternate path without disrupting the control session. For critical infrastructure such as electrical substations or pipeline control stations, uninterrupted communication is essential, and SCTP enables this without requiring complex application-level logic or external failover systems.

SCTP's message-oriented nature aligns perfectly with the structure of SCADA communication. Industrial protocols such as DNP3, IEC 60870-5-104, or Modbus over TCP rely on discrete packets of data representing commands, sensor readings, or status updates. These messages need to be delivered whole and interpreted correctly, without being broken up or merged as can happen in stream-based protocols like TCP. With SCTP, each data unit is preserved as a message from sender to receiver, ensuring that the control logic on either end receives clean and consistent data for processing. This minimizes parsing complexity, reduces the chance of misinterpretation, and makes the system more robust to unexpected message boundaries or fragmentation errors.

Multistreaming is another powerful feature of SCTP that enhances performance in SCADA systems. Within a single SCTP association, multiple logical streams can carry independent sequences of data. For a SCADA master controlling hundreds of devices across different facilities, each stream can be assigned to a different device, process, or message type. For example, alarms could be transmitted over one stream, telemetry over another, and operator commands over a third. This separation prevents delays in one type of data from affecting others. In TCP-based systems, a single delayed or lost packet can block all subsequent data until the issue is resolved. SCTP avoids this by allowing each stream to operate independently, which is crucial when critical alarms or control actions must not be delayed by routine polling or logging messages.

Partial reliability is also highly relevant in industrial applications where time-sensitive data loses value if delayed. Many SCADA systems sample sensor data at regular intervals and send these readings to a central control room. If a value is not received in time, it may no longer be useful for operational decisions. SCTP's Partial Reliability Extension allows applications to assign expiration criteria to messages. If a message cannot be delivered within a defined time window, it is discarded instead of retransmitted. This ensures that network and processing resources are focused on delivering the most relevant data, avoiding congestion caused by outdated information. In applications like turbine monitoring or chemical process control, where readings must reflect the current state accurately, this feature allows for real-time performance without sacrificing network efficiency.

SCTP also provides robust congestion control and flow management mechanisms, which are critical in networks shared by multiple SCADA nodes and other operational technologies. The protocol's selective acknowledgment mechanism ensures that only missing data is retransmitted, reducing unnecessary traffic and helping maintain consistent throughput. Its congestion control algorithms adapt dynamically to network conditions, minimizing the likelihood of packet loss and reducing jitter. This is important in industrial control networks where jitter or excessive retransmissions can lead to command execution delays or false alarms.

Security is an increasingly important aspect of SCADA and industrial systems as they become more interconnected and exposed to external networks. SCTP includes several built-in features that help secure communication without relying entirely on external layers. The protocol uses verification tags and a four-way handshake to prevent spoofing and blind attacks. The optional use of authentication chunks enables message integrity and source verification, ensuring that only trusted peers can communicate. These features enhance the overall security posture of SCADA systems and support compliance with cybersecurity frameworks such as NERC CIP, IEC 62443, and ISO/IEC 27019.

In mobile and wireless industrial networks, such as those used in utility trucks, trains, or pipeline inspections, SCTP's dynamic address reconfiguration provides additional flexibility. When an endpoint moves between network zones or changes interfaces, SCTP can update the peer with new IP addresses and continue communication over a different path without resetting the session. This allows field units to maintain persistent connections to central control systems as they move or reconnect, enabling real-time updates and continuous control even during network transitions.

Integration of SCTP into SCADA architectures is facilitated by the protocol's compatibility with IPv4 and IPv6, as well as its support for encapsulation over UDP when NAT traversal or firewall compatibility is needed. This allows SCTP-based systems to operate across various network topologies, including legacy LANs, modern IP backbones, satellite links, and 5G networks. SCTP-aware firewalls and routers can be configured to monitor and prioritize SCADA traffic, enhancing quality of service and ensuring that control and monitoring messages receive appropriate treatment.

Operational monitoring of SCTP sessions also aids in maintaining system availability and diagnosing faults. SCTP provides detailed feedback through control chunks such as HEARTBEAT, SACK, and SHUTDOWN, which can be logged and analyzed to track network health, detect performance bottlenecks, and anticipate failures. These capabilities are essential for operators managing critical infrastructure who need real-time visibility into communication reliability and efficiency.

SCTP's capabilities align with the demands of next-generation industrial systems that are increasingly digitized, distributed, and expected to operate autonomously or semi-autonomously. As SCADA evolves to incorporate more edge intelligence, remote analytics, and cloud-based coordination, the transport layer must be robust, flexible, and adaptable. SCTP offers a strong foundation for this transformation, delivering dependable connectivity, orderly and efficient data handling, and the resilience needed to operate industrial systems safely and effectively under all conditions.

Comparative Benchmarking with Other Protocols

In the evolving landscape of transport protocols, selecting the right one requires a detailed understanding of how each performs under various conditions and application requirements. The Stream Control Transmission Protocol has emerged as a versatile option, offering a blend of reliability, efficiency, and flexibility. To appreciate its advantages and limitations, it is essential to benchmark SCTP against other commonly used transport protocols, particularly Transmission Control Protocol and User Datagram Protocol. Comparative benchmarking involves measuring throughput, latency, loss handling, connection management, congestion behavior, and adaptability across different environments and traffic patterns.

TCP is the most widely adopted transport protocol for reliable data transmission on the internet. It guarantees in-order, reliable delivery using a byte-stream model, making it suitable for applications where data integrity and sequence are essential. However, TCP has long been criticized for its inability to handle diverse application data types efficiently. One of the most significant limitations in TCP is head-of-line blocking, where a single lost or delayed segment can hold up all subsequent data. This rigid ordering constraint becomes a performance bottleneck in scenarios with multiple concurrent data streams, such as multimedia transmission or real-time control applications. SCTP overcomes this with multistreaming, enabling multiple independent logical streams within a single association. In benchmark tests simulating multiple simultaneous flows, SCTP demonstrates lower latency and improved throughput in applications where message types can be processed independently.

UDP represents the opposite end of the spectrum. It is connectionless, does not guarantee delivery or ordering, and introduces minimal overhead. For applications like voice over IP, online gaming, and video conferencing, UDP's simplicity provides superior performance when speed is prioritized over reliability. However, UDP offloads responsibility for error handling and ordering to the application layer, increasing implementation complexity. Benchmarking reveals that while UDP maintains the lowest latency in optimal conditions, it suffers dramatically under packet loss or jitter. SCTP, in contrast, provides a middle ground. It delivers reliable and optionally ordered messages with built-in congestion control and retransmission, all while preserving application-layer message boundaries. In comparative benchmarks involving lossy network simulations, SCTP consistently outperforms UDP in data integrity and recovers from loss more efficiently than TCP due to selective acknowledgments and partial reliability options.

A key aspect of benchmarking SCTP involves its behavior under congestion. TCP uses congestion avoidance algorithms like slow start, congestion avoidance, and fast recovery. SCTP implements similar mechanisms but with more granularity and efficiency. It supports selective acknowledgment, allowing precise retransmission of only the missing data chunks, and has built-in path management that enables dynamic failover in multihomed environments. In congestion simulations where bandwidth fluctuates or packet loss increases due to network overload, SCTP maintains a more stable throughput compared to TCP, which often drops drastically before recovering. This stability is crucial for maintaining quality of service in real-time and critical systems.

Connection management is another critical factor in transport protocol performance. TCP uses a three-way handshake, which makes it vulnerable to SYN flood attacks, as it allocates state for each handshake attempt. SCTP introduces a four-way handshake using a cookie mechanism, allowing the server to remain stateless until the client's legitimacy is verified. Benchmarks involving connection attempts per second show that SCTP resists denial-of-service attacks more effectively, maintaining responsiveness even under high-volume connection floods, whereas TCP quickly exhausts resources under similar conditions. UDP, lacking any connection mechanism, does not suffer from such issues but is entirely dependent on application-level authentication and session tracking.

In terms of resource consumption, TCP and SCTP both maintain state for each connection, including sequence numbers, timers, and buffers. SCTP's state model is more complex due to its support for multiple streams and paths, which can increase memory and CPU usage in constrained environments. However, in scenarios involving numerous short-lived connections, such as web services or signaling exchanges, SCTP's stateless initiation and path failover offer long-term efficiency by reducing reconnection overhead and preventing application-layer retries. Benchmarks involving thousands of concurrent connections demonstrate that SCTP scales comparably to TCP while offering improved resilience and message handling flexibility.

The multihoming capability of SCTP is another significant differentiator. In failover tests where network interfaces are intentionally disconnected, SCTP can detect path failures using heartbeat messages and switch to alternate paths without dropping the session. TCP and UDP, by contrast, require a complete reconnection or must rely on application-level support to manage interface changes. This difference is most apparent in mobile or high-availability environments, where SCTP's uninterrupted session continuity provides tangible performance benefits in terms of user experience and operational uptime. Benchmarks measuring session continuity across link failures consistently show SCTP as superior, with near-instantaneous failover and no data loss during transitions.

In applications involving structured messaging, such as signaling protocols or real-time control messages, SCTP's message boundary preservation becomes a critical advantage. TCP's byte-stream nature requires additional framing logic, increasing both latency and complexity. Benchmarks comparing parsing speed and message integrity under variable loads reveal that SCTP simplifies and accelerates message decoding by delivering well-formed messages directly to the application. UDP, while message-oriented, lacks reliability, making SCTP the preferred choice where both structure and delivery assurance are required.

SCTP also performs well in secure communication benchmarking. When encapsulated in DTLS over UDP, it offers end-to-end security compatible with NAT traversal, a feature leveraged in WebRTC and peer-to-peer applications. TCP traditionally uses TLS for security, which adds overhead and latency during handshake and encryption. Benchmarks comparing DTLS-SCTP and TLS-TCP configurations indicate that while TLS startup is faster in well-optimized implementations, SCTP's message granularity results in better sustained throughput for secure messaging applications.

Energy efficiency is an emerging benchmark criterion, especially for mobile and IoT applications. Due to its retransmission efficiency and ability to discard stale data using partial reliability, SCTP consumes less bandwidth and requires fewer CPU cycles in certain real-time data delivery scenarios. Benchmarks measuring energy usage per message in low-power wireless environments show that SCTP can be more efficient than TCP, particularly when partial reliability is enabled and stale retransmissions are avoided.

While SCTP's implementation is less ubiquitous than TCP and UDP, its performance characteristics make it a strong candidate in environments where reliability, ordering, and connection resilience are critical. Through benchmarking under diverse conditions—ranging from lossy networks and high-connection volumes to secure environments and mobile transitions—SCTP demonstrates a unique ability to balance robustness with flexibility. Although it may require additional configuration or support in legacy systems, its advantages in performance, especially under stress, make SCTP a valuable asset in transport-layer design and a compelling alternative to more established protocols.

Tuning SCTP for Low Latency

Latency is a critical factor in a wide range of applications, from real-time voice and video communications to industrial control systems and financial trading platforms. Low latency is essential for ensuring responsiveness, maintaining synchronization, and enabling rapid decision-making. The Stream Control Transmission Protocol, while designed to be a robust and feature-rich transport protocol, can also be tuned effectively to minimize latency without sacrificing its reliability and flexibility. Proper tuning of SCTP involves understanding its internal mechanisms and adjusting various parameters related to buffering, retransmission, path management, and delivery modes to align with the specific demands of latency-sensitive systems.

One of the key aspects to address when optimizing SCTP for low latency is the management of retransmission behaviors. Unlike TCP, which delays retransmissions until the expiry of a conservative timeout, SCTP provides mechanisms for faster recovery through selective acknowledgments and gap detection. The use of the Selective Acknowledgment (SACK) chunk allows the receiver to report exactly which chunks have been received and which are missing. SCTP then uses this information to perform fast retransmissions without waiting for the retransmission timer to expire. To further reduce latency, the retransmission timeout (RTO) parameters can be tuned to be more aggressive. This includes reducing the initial RTO value, enabling exponential backoff limitations, and lowering the maximum RTO threshold. By shortening these intervals, SCTP becomes more responsive in detecting and recovering from lost data.

Another powerful feature that contributes to latency reduction is the support for Partial Reliability. SCTP allows the application to specify messages that do not require full reliability. These can include telemetry data, real-time status updates, or time-sensitive control commands. Using the Partial Reliability Extension, SCTP can be instructed to skip retransmissions of certain messages if they exceed a time threshold or a maximum number of retransmission attempts. This reduces the protocol's effort spent on delivering data that would no longer be useful by the time it arrives, and instead prioritizes the transmission of newer, more relevant information. This mechanism is especially important in systems such as video conferencing, where a delayed video frame has no value once it falls behind the current playback time.

Buffering strategies must also be carefully considered when tuning SCTP for latency. Large buffers introduce delays, as data must accumulate before transmission or processing occurs. By minimizing buffer sizes and avoiding unnecessary queuing, data can be processed and sent more promptly. Operating systems often use large socket buffers by default to maximize throughput, but these settings can work against low-latency goals. Applications using SCTP should configure smaller send and receive buffers through socket options, such as

SO_SNDBUF and SO_RCVBUF, and use SCTP_INITMSG to specify the number of streams and maximum attempts appropriate to the expected traffic. Reducing buffer size forces the protocol to transmit immediately rather than waiting for additional data to fill the buffer, thereby reducing send delays.

The way data is structured and transmitted also affects latency. SCTP's chunk-based message framing supports the interleaving of messages from different streams, reducing blocking effects between streams. When multiple streams are used in parallel, SCTP can prioritize urgent data from one stream even if another stream is handling a large message. This prevents long messages from monopolizing the connection and delaying smaller, high-priority updates. Enabling stream interleaving and configuring stream priorities allows developers to ensure that important messages such as control commands or alerts are delivered with minimal delay, regardless of other ongoing transmissions.

Path management in multihomed environments also plays a critical role in tuning SCTP for low latency. SCTP supports multihoming, which allows endpoints to maintain multiple paths between them, typically over different network interfaces. By default, SCTP selects a primary path and uses others only for failover. However, in low-latency tuning, it may be advantageous to dynamically assess path quality and switch to the path with the lowest round-trip time. This can be achieved by analyzing the heartbeat acknowledgments and delay metrics reported by each path. More advanced implementations can perform active path probing to continuously monitor all paths and reroute traffic based on current performance. Selecting the optimal path reduces propagation delays and ensures more consistent timing, which is critical in interactive or tightly synchronized systems.

SCTP's control of delivery ordering is another area where latency can be optimized. For messages that do not require strict ordering, such as mouse movements in a remote desktop session or GPS coordinates in a tracking system, unordered delivery can be enabled at the stream level. This allows each message to be delivered as soon as it is received and validated, bypassing the need to wait for earlier messages that may have been delayed or lost. By enabling unordered delivery using the SCTP_UNORDERED flag, the application gains lower delivery latency at the cost of sequence guarantees, which is acceptable in many real-time use cases.

Congestion control mechanisms, while essential for fairness and network stability, can also introduce latency when not properly configured. SCTP uses a congestion window similar to TCP's, which limits the rate at which new data can be sent. In low-latency configurations, the initial congestion window size can be increased to allow more data to be sent early in the connection, and the congestion control algorithms can be selected or adjusted based on the expected network conditions. Some implementations support alternate algorithms that are more aggressive in utilizing available bandwidth, which can be beneficial in dedicated or high-performance networks where loss is low and delays are minimal.

Tuning SCTP for low latency also involves monitoring and feedback loops. Logging retransmission times, round-trip delays, chunk arrival times, and buffer levels allows developers and operators to observe the protocol's real-time performance and adjust parameters accordingly. Tools like Wireshark provide detailed insight into SCTP associations, including chunk types, delays between acknowledgments, and path state changes. This visibility is invaluable when troubleshooting latency spikes or verifying the effectiveness of tuning adjustments.

Application behavior also influences SCTP's latency performance. Applications must avoid blocking calls that delay reading from the socket or writing data into the association. Using non-blocking I/O or asynchronous frameworks ensures that the application keeps pace with the transport layer's responsiveness. When combined with a well-tuned SCTP stack, this allows for end-to-end latency reductions that are significant enough to impact user experience or operational precision.

By thoughtfully tuning its configuration and leveraging its advanced features, SCTP can achieve latency performance that rivals or exceeds traditional transport protocols while maintaining its rich reliability and failover capabilities. It offers a versatile and powerful foundation for real-time systems that need both speed and assurance, and with the right tuning strategies, it adapts effectively to a wide range of low-latency environments.

Adaptive Streaming and SCTP

Adaptive streaming is an essential technique in the delivery of multimedia content over the internet, particularly for video and audio services where network conditions can vary dramatically. It allows clients to adjust the quality of the stream in real time based on available bandwidth, latency, and packet loss, thereby ensuring uninterrupted playback and optimal user experience. Traditional protocols like HTTP over TCP have been widely used for adaptive streaming through standards like MPEG-DASH and HLS. However, these protocols have inherent limitations, especially with latency and rebuffering, as TCP enforces strict ordering and retransmission policies that can delay the delivery of useful data. The Stream Control Transmission Protocol offers several features that make it a promising transport layer for adaptive streaming, particularly in use cases requiring real-time responsiveness, dynamic quality switching, and reliable data delivery without the penalties of head-of-line blocking.

One of the primary advantages of SCTP for adaptive streaming is its support for multistreaming. In a multimedia streaming session, different types of data are typically transmitted, including video frames, audio samples, subtitles, metadata, and control messages. SCTP enables these data types to be sent on separate logical streams within a single association, with each stream maintaining its own ordering and reliability policy. This separation ensures that a delay or loss affecting one type of data does not stall the delivery of others. For instance, if a large video frame is lost and awaiting retransmission, it does not block the delivery of subsequent audio packets or subtitle data. This capability is essential for adaptive streaming, where timely delivery of lower bitrate streams during congestion is more valuable than waiting for higher quality segments that may never arrive in time.

SCTP also provides message-oriented delivery, which aligns well with the discrete structure of video and audio chunks used in adaptive streaming. Each segment or frame can be encapsulated as a single SCTP message, maintaining its boundaries and reducing parsing complexity. Unlike TCP, which requires application-level framing due to its stream-based nature, SCTP delivers whole messages as defined by the application, improving efficiency and reducing the risk of misinterpretation. This is especially beneficial when switching between different quality levels, as each quality segment is a self-contained unit that can be easily managed by the transport layer.

The partial reliability extension of SCTP is particularly advantageous in adaptive streaming scenarios. Real-time media content has limited usefulness if delayed, and retransmitting outdated data wastes valuable bandwidth. SCTP allows applications to define time or retransmission limits for individual messages. If a message cannot be delivered within the defined constraints, it is discarded. This behavior closely matches the needs of adaptive streaming clients, which frequently abandon pending requests for higher quality segments in favor of newer, lower quality segments that can be delivered more quickly. By avoiding unnecessary retransmissions, SCTP helps maintain smooth playback and reduces the risk of buffering.

SCTP's congestion control and flow management mechanisms contribute to its suitability for adaptive streaming. The protocol dynamically adjusts the sending rate based on network feedback, including selective acknowledgments and round-trip time estimates. These controls prevent the sender from overwhelming the network while maximizing throughput. When network conditions degrade, SCTP naturally reduces its sending rate, prompting the adaptive streaming algorithm to request lower bitrate segments. Conversely, when conditions improve, higher bitrate segments can be delivered without needing to renegotiate the transport association or switch protocols.

Multihoming is another SCTP feature that enhances adaptive streaming performance in devices with multiple network interfaces. Many modern devices can connect simultaneously to Wi-Fi, cellular, and other networks. SCTP allows an endpoint to bind multiple IP addresses to the same association, enabling seamless path failover and redundancy. If the primary path experiences degradation or failure, SCTP can switch to an alternate path without dropping the session or requiring renegotiation. In streaming applications, this ensures uninterrupted playback even when the user moves between networks or encounters intermittent connectivity issues.

In the context of client-server or peer-to-peer streaming architectures, SCTP's support for NAT traversal through UDP encapsulation and integration with ICE makes it feasible for use in consumer environments. Many adaptive streaming applications, particularly browser-based or mobile apps, must function across NATs and firewalls. SCTP encapsulated in UDP, combined with ICE and STUN, can establish reliable paths through these barriers, making it deployable at scale alongside existing WebRTC-based media solutions.

From a development standpoint, SCTP can be customized to align with the specific needs of adaptive streaming platforms. Developers can configure per-stream delivery modes, adjust retransmission strategies, and prioritize control messages such as segment requests or buffer status updates. These capabilities allow the transport layer to work in harmony with the adaptive bitrate logic, ensuring that decisions made at the application level are supported by efficient, intelligent transport behavior.

SCTP's ability to handle both reliable and partially reliable delivery within the same session is particularly well suited for hybrid streaming approaches, where critical control messages or metadata must be delivered reliably while media content is treated with less strict delivery requirements. This flexibility reduces the need for multiple protocols and simplifies application architecture. Additionally, by maintaining persistent associations across streaming sessions, SCTP can reduce connection overhead and latency compared to protocols that require frequent handshakes and renegotiations.

Monitoring and diagnostics in adaptive streaming systems are crucial for maintaining quality of experience. SCTP provides detailed feedback about path performance, chunk delivery status, and retransmission events. These insights can be used to fine-tune bitrate selection algorithms and identify bottlenecks in the delivery chain. Tools like Wireshark can capture and analyze SCTP traffic, enabling operators and developers to visualize stream behaviors, detect anomalies, and verify that tuning parameters are functioning as expected.

As streaming continues to evolve toward ultra-low latency, high-resolution content, and interactive experiences such as cloud gaming and virtual reality, the transport protocol must be able to support increasingly demanding requirements. SCTP offers a future-proof foundation for adaptive streaming by combining resilience, efficiency, and application-level control. Its features directly address the limitations of traditional transport protocols and enable streaming platforms to deliver smoother, more responsive, and higher-quality media to users across diverse network environments.

SCTP Simulation Tools and Testbeds

Simulating network protocols before deployment is a crucial step in ensuring that performance, reliability, and scalability requirements are met under a variety of conditions. For the Stream Control Transmission Protocol, simulation tools and testbeds serve a vital role in evaluating its behavior in diverse real-world and theoretical environments. SCTP, with its complex set of features such as multistreaming, multihoming, partial reliability, and congestion control, must be thoroughly tested to understand how these mechanisms perform under stress, variable latency, jitter, packet loss, and failover scenarios. Because SCTP is often deployed in critical systems, including telecom signaling, industrial networks, and real-time media applications, the use of advanced simulation platforms becomes not only useful but necessary for validation and optimization.

One of the most widely used environments for simulating network protocols is the ns-3 simulator. As a discrete-event network simulator, ns-3 allows researchers and engineers to model complex topologies and simulate SCTP behavior at both endpoint and network levels. The SCTP module in ns-3 supports a substantial subset of the protocol's functionality, including stream handling, congestion control, and chunk-based message delivery. Through ns-3, developers can model multihomed endpoints and study failover behavior when one or more network paths go down. They can also configure traffic generators to simulate application workloads such as voice, video, and control signals. Ns-3 provides detailed trace logs and packet captures, enabling fine-grained analysis of SCTP associations, retransmissions, path switches, and congestion window behavior over time.

OMNeT++ is another prominent simulation platform often used in academic and industrial research to study SCTP. Unlike ns-3, OMNeT++ provides a component-based architecture with a visual simulation environment. Its extensible framework supports modular protocol stack modeling, making it ideal for studying interactions between SCTP and other network layers such as IP, UDP, or application protocols. The INET framework for OMNeT++ includes SCTP support and provides capabilities for testing scenarios involving partial reliability, multistreaming performance, and stream prioritization. Researchers can simulate high-latency satellite links, mobile networks with intermittent connectivity, or complex cloud deployments with dynamic IP addressing. The event-driven nature of OMNeT++ also makes it suitable for modeling behavior in systems where timing and synchronization are critical, such as SCADA networks or live media streaming.

Beyond simulation platforms, emulation environments such as Mininet and CORE allow for real-time experimentation with SCTP using actual protocol implementations. These environments use virtual network interfaces and namespaces to create realistic network topologies on a single machine or distributed testbed. SCTP stacks within Linux or FreeBSD can be used in these emulated networks to observe how the protocol behaves under specific configurations. For example, developers can test the impact of different retransmission timeout values, stream configurations, or authentication parameters. Emulation testbeds are particularly useful for verifying interoperability between different SCTP implementations, as well as for evaluating real applications that use SCTP under controlled but realistic network conditions.

In more sophisticated research and development environments, SCTP is tested using hardware-in-the-loop systems and hybrid testbeds that combine physical and virtual infrastructure. These setups are often used in telecommunications, where vendors need to test SCTP under the 3GPP-defined control plane interfaces such as S1-MME and X2 in LTE or NGAP in 5G. Testbeds may include commercial signaling equipment, radio access simulators, and EPC core components integrated with traffic generators and protocol analyzers. Using this setup, engineers can validate SCTP performance under high loads, stress test path failover mechanisms, and verify protocol compliance with standards. This type of testing is especially critical in carrier-grade environments, where SCTP must maintain thousands of concurrent associations and support near-zero downtime.

Another valuable tool for SCTP testing is Wireshark, a packet analysis tool that includes full support for dissecting SCTP packets. In both simulated and real environments, Wireshark allows users to examine each chunk, track retransmissions, monitor heartbeats, and follow the progression of the association lifecycle. When combined with logging tools or telemetry frameworks, Wireshark helps correlate application-level events with transport-layer behaviors. This is crucial for debugging latency issues, verifying message ordering, or identifying anomalies in congestion control.

For dynamic and large-scale experiments, cloud-based testbeds such as those provided by GENI or Emulab offer flexible and powerful platforms for SCTP experimentation. These platforms allow users to reserve compute and network resources, deploy custom operating system images with SCTP support, and run experiments across geographically distributed nodes. Such testbeds are useful for examining SCTP behavior in wide-area network conditions, including asymmetric routes, variable delays, and cross-traffic interference. Experiments conducted in these environments can replicate production-scale scenarios and generate reproducible results that inform deployment strategies.

SCTP simulation and testbed environments are also valuable for evaluating proposed extensions or modifications to the protocol. For instance, researchers investigating enhancements to SCTP's congestion control mechanisms or new authentication methods can implement their changes in ns-3 or OMNeT++, run simulations under varied network conditions, and compare performance metrics against baseline behavior. These tools allow for iterative development, where hypotheses can be tested and refined before any changes are considered for standardization or inclusion in production stacks.

The integration of automated testing frameworks with SCTP testbeds is another area of growing importance. By scripting test scenarios and integrating them into continuous integration pipelines, developers can automatically validate protocol compliance and performance regressions as new changes are introduced. This is particularly important in open-source SCTP stacks where community contributions must be rigorously tested. Automated testing also facilitates long-term monitoring of SCTP stability across different kernel versions or operating system distributions.

As SCTP adoption expands into new domains such as WebRTC, Internet of Things, and mission-critical control networks, the role of simulation and testbeds becomes even more central. Each application domain presents unique challenges in terms of latency, reliability, scalability, and security. Simulation tools and test environments allow developers to adapt SCTP configurations, validate performance under domain-specific constraints, and ensure that the protocol delivers its promised benefits. By enabling structured, repeatable, and observable experimentation, these tools contribute directly to SCTP's reliability as a transport layer for the future of real-time communications.

Wireshark and SCTP Packet Analysis

Analyzing the behavior of the Stream Control Transmission Protocol in live networks or controlled test environments requires powerful and flexible tools that can inspect traffic at the packet level. Wireshark, a widely used network protocol analyzer, plays a critical role in understanding how SCTP functions under various conditions. Whether for debugging, performance optimization, security auditing, or educational purposes, Wireshark provides deep visibility into SCTP communications, allowing users to capture, dissect, and interpret every aspect of the protocol's operation. Its ability to decode SCTP chunks, follow multistreaming sequences, and track connection states in real time makes it an essential instrument for developers, testers, and network engineers working with SCTP.

Wireshark supports SCTP natively, and its dissector can interpret each component of an SCTP packet, beginning with the common header. The SCTP common header includes fields such as the source and destination port numbers, verification tag, and checksum. The verification tag is especially important for security and association integrity, as it ensures that the packet belongs to the expected session.

When observing captured packets in Wireshark, users can immediately see the verification tag value and compare it with those from earlier in the session to detect spoofed or invalid packets.

Following the header, Wireshark breaks down the contents of each SCTP chunk. Chunks are the fundamental unit of SCTP communication, each encapsulating control information, data, or other operational messages. Wireshark decodes each chunk type, displaying it with a clear label such as INIT, INIT-ACK, COOKIE-ECHO, COOKIE-ACK, DATA, SACK, HEARTBEAT, HEARTBEAT-ACK, or SHUTDOWN. This allows users to track the progression of the SCTP association, from the initial handshake through active data transmission and into the teardown process. Each chunk is presented with detailed field values, including stream identifiers, transmission sequence numbers, and flags such as unordered delivery or beginning and end-of-message indicators.

One of the most powerful features of Wireshark for SCTP analysis is the ability to follow a stream. While TCP streams are displayed as continuous byte streams, SCTP streams maintain their message boundaries, which Wireshark preserves in its visualizations. When following an SCTP stream, Wireshark shows individual messages and their associated metadata, such as stream ID and sequence number. This is invaluable for verifying that messages arrive in order, are not duplicated, and are not lost. In multistreaming scenarios, Wireshark allows users to distinguish traffic belonging to different streams within a single association, making it easier to detect misrouted or missequenced data.

SCTP's Selective Acknowledgment (SACK) mechanism is also clearly presented in Wireshark. Each SACK chunk includes the cumulative TSN acknowledged and a list of gap acknowledgment blocks and duplicate TSNs. These elements are crucial for understanding retransmission behavior, detecting packet loss, and measuring round-trip times. Wireshark displays these values in a readable format, enabling users to assess how well the sender and receiver are managing data delivery and acknowledgment. Analysts can determine whether retransmissions are occurring due to actual loss or simply as a result of delayed acknowledgment. By correlating SACKs with the corresponding DATA chunks, one can also track latency and infer congestion levels.

Wireshark also supports the dissection of SCTP parameters exchanged during the initial association setup. INIT and INIT-ACK chunks often contain a list of supported parameters, such as the number of outbound and inbound streams, supported extensions like PR-SCTP or authentication, and optional address lists in multihomed configurations. Observing these parameters helps verify that the endpoints have negotiated the intended capabilities and that the association reflects the expected configuration. This is especially useful in troubleshooting problems where one side is not respecting the desired stream count or fails to recognize optional features.

In multihoming environments, where SCTP can use multiple network paths between endpoints, Wireshark captures each path's usage and heartbeat messages. Heartbeat chunks are periodically sent over alternate paths to test their reachability, and Heartbeat-ACK chunks confirm the path is active. Wireshark logs these interactions and timestamps them, enabling engineers to detect link degradation, delayed responses, or failover events. When path failover occurs, the traffic flow can be observed moving from one IP address to another, with all the related signaling messages visible in sequence. This capability is especially important in environments that depend on high availability and seamless failover, such as telecom signaling systems or mission-critical industrial control networks.

When SCTP is used in encapsulated modes, such as SCTP over DTLS over UDP in WebRTC, Wireshark is still capable of analyzing the protocol if the session keys are available and decryption is enabled. While encrypted packets cannot be interpreted without keys, the outer layers still reveal metadata such as source and destination ports, packet sizes, and transport timing. This enables analysts to study connection patterns, latency behavior, and handshake timings even when the payload is secured. In secure environments, these insights can help detect performance bottlenecks or uncover potential misconfigurations in encryption layers.

Wireshark's filtering and search capabilities enhance SCTP analysis by allowing users to isolate specific chunks, stream identifiers, or even errors. Filters such as sctp.chunk_type == 0x03 for SACK chunks or sctp.stream_id == 5 for a specific stream allow precise navigation of large capture files. Combined with time-based filters and I/O graphs, users can generate visual representations of retransmission rates, throughput over time, or latency between chunks. These visualizations help communicate findings to stakeholders and support data-driven decision-making in development and operations.

In diagnostic scenarios, Wireshark can expose unexpected behavior, such as duplicate DATA chunks indicating unnecessary retransmissions, or invalid sequence numbers suggesting corruption or implementation errors. Wireshark flags malformed packets and protocol violations, helping developers quickly locate bugs in custom SCTP implementations or misbehaving third-party stacks. It also helps confirm compliance with RFC specifications, such as correct ordering of control chunks or presence of mandatory fields.

The integration of Wireshark with scripting tools like Tshark and command-line automation enables batch processing of capture files, which is useful for regression testing and continuous integration environments. Developers can write scripts to analyze specific SCTP metrics across multiple test runs, automatically generate summaries, and flag anomalies. This approach brings repeatability and scalability to SCTP testing efforts and supports long-term monitoring in production systems.

Wireshark serves as a critical enabler for understanding and mastering SCTP behavior at a granular level. By providing full visibility into packet contents, timing, sequencing, and control flow, it empowers engineers to debug complex problems, optimize performance, ensure protocol compliance, and build systems that leverage SCTP's capabilities to their fullest. Its ability to represent the nuances of SCTP communication makes it an indispensable tool in any workflow involving the analysis, development, or operation of SCTP-based applications and networks.

Debugging and Tracing SCTP Connections

Debugging and tracing SCTP connections is a crucial part of developing, deploying, and maintaining applications and systems that rely on this protocol for communication. Due to its rich set of features and complex behaviors—such as multihoming, multistreaming, chunk-based message structure, partial reliability, and built-in failover—SCTP presents unique challenges and opportunities for diagnostics. Whether an SCTP connection is failing to establish, experiencing data loss, misordering chunks, or behaving unexpectedly under load, effective debugging and tracing strategies allow engineers to identify and resolve problems with precision and efficiency.

The first step in debugging SCTP is enabling comprehensive logging within the SCTP stack being used. Most SCTP implementations in modern operating systems, such as those found in Linux, FreeBSD, or Windows, provide configurable debugging interfaces. In Linux, the SCTP module includes a set of debug flags that can be controlled through kernel parameters or sysctl interfaces. These flags activate logging of various events, including association setup, chunk transmission, acknowledgment handling, and retransmission timeouts. Logs generated through dmesg or system journal tools provide insights into how the protocol is progressing at each step and can highlight where associations fail, whether due to timeout, authentication failure, or malformed parameters.

Tracing tools that operate at the network level are also indispensable. tcpdump is a lightweight and powerful tool used to capture SCTP traffic at the packet level. By invoking tcpdump with filters such as proto sctp or specifying specific ports used by SCTP associations, engineers can capture raw traffic for later inspection. These capture files can then be analyzed using Wireshark, which decodes SCTP packets in detail. In Wireshark, engineers can observe the flow of control and data chunks, monitor retransmissions, examine Selective Acknowledgment chunks, and visualize the handshake process. The ability to track sequence numbers and stream identifiers over time is critical for debugging issues related to message delivery, ordering, and chunk interleaving.

One of the challenges in debugging SCTP connections is understanding the implications of its multistreaming feature. Because data streams are independent within a single association, issues such as blocked streams or delayed delivery may not be obvious when only observing high-level application behavior. Debugging at this level requires visibility into individual stream identifiers and their sequence numbers. Tools like Wireshark provide stream-specific filtering, allowing engineers to isolate specific message flows. Logs from the SCTP stack can also include per-stream status, including transmission windows, pending acknowledgments, and retransmission queues.

Multihoming adds another layer of complexity to debugging SCTP connections. When multiple IP addresses are bound to an endpoint, SCTP dynamically selects paths for data transmission and performs failover when one path becomes unresponsive. Problems may arise when one path silently drops packets, misroutes them, or becomes unstable. In such cases, heartbeat chunks and their acknowledgments become essential for tracing path health. Engineers must monitor heartbeat exchanges and identify which path transitions are occurring. When debugging failover scenarios, attention must be paid to the timing of the heartbeat intervals, retransmission attempts, and the thresholds that determine when a path is declared down. Misconfiguration of these parameters can lead to premature failover, delayed recovery, or even unnecessary path flapping.

In environments with firewalls or NAT devices, SCTP connections may fail to establish or may appear unstable. Debugging in these scenarios requires careful examination of initial handshake packets, particularly the INIT and INIT-ACK chunks, and ensuring that cookies are properly echoed and validated. NAT devices that are not SCTP-aware can interfere with path integrity, especially when alternate paths or dynamic IP addresses are used. Engineers should verify that SCTP encapsulation in UDP is supported and properly configured when NAT traversal is required. Diagnostic logs can reveal mismatches in verification tags, malformed cookies, or rejections due to unsupported parameters.

For application developers using the SCTP socket API, debugging often involves checking return values of system calls and interpreting error codes. SCTP-specific socket options such as SCTP_STATUS,

SCTP_GET_PEER_ADDRS, and SCTP_GET_STREAMS provide runtime information about the state of the association, the active streams, and the available peer addresses. Developers can use these options to query the status of the connection, inspect congestion windows, and determine if messages are being delayed due to buffer overflows or congestion control. When integrated into application logs, this data provides visibility into the transport layer from the application's point of view, aiding in correlation with network-level traces.

Real-time tracing tools such as SystemTap, eBPF, or DTrace allow for kernel-level instrumentation of SCTP activity without requiring full packet captures. These tools can attach to specific kernel functions and record when associations are created, when chunks are sent or received, and when timeouts or errors occur. This level of tracing is particularly useful in performance-critical environments where minimal intrusion is desired or where traditional packet capture is impractical. For example, eBPF programs can trace retransmission timers and log the exact cause of a retransmission, revealing whether it was due to packet loss or delayed acknowledgment.

Integration of SCTP debugging and tracing into automated test environments is also critical for long-term maintainability. Regression testing frameworks can include SCTP association validation, failure injection, and stress testing with monitoring hooks that capture performance metrics, chunk flow statistics, and path selection behavior. These automated tests help detect bugs early, ensure that failover mechanisms work as intended, and verify compliance with protocol standards under controlled conditions.

Finally, effective debugging of SCTP connections depends on a strong understanding of the protocol's architecture. Engineers must be familiar with the handshake process, the structure of chunks, the interaction between streams, the purpose of verification tags, and the conditions under which each type of chunk is sent. Debugging is not just about observing what went wrong but understanding the expected behavior and recognizing when that behavior deviates. The combination of network captures, kernel logs, socket-level status checks, and structured instrumentation provides a comprehensive toolkit for diagnosing and resolving SCTP-related issues in any environment.

SCTP offers powerful capabilities that make it a preferred choice in systems where reliability, ordering, and resilience are essential. However, its complexity demands equally powerful tools and disciplined debugging practices. Through structured tracing and detailed analysis, engineers can unlock the full potential of SCTP, ensuring stable, high-performance connections across a wide range of applications and infrastructures.

SCTP in Mission-Critical Systems

Mission-critical systems are defined by their requirement for absolute reliability, high availability, and continuous operation under all circumstances. These systems are often deployed in sectors such as aerospace, defense, energy, healthcare, emergency response, and industrial automation, where even brief communication failures can result in severe financial losses, safety hazards, or irreversible operational damage. In this context, the transport protocol that carries control messages, telemetry data, and operational commands must not only be dependable but must also exhibit resilience to failure, support real-time performance, and offer mechanisms for fault recovery. The Stream Control Transmission Protocol is uniquely equipped to serve this role due to its robust feature set, which was engineered specifically to handle complex and sensitive communication requirements that exceed the capabilities of legacy transport protocols like TCP and UDP.

One of the foundational features that makes SCTP ideal for mission-critical systems is its multihoming capability. In such systems, redundancy is not a luxury but a necessity. SCTP allows each endpoint to bind to multiple IP addresses simultaneously, creating several potential paths between communicating nodes. This ensures that if the primary network interface, router, or link fails, the protocol can seamlessly reroute data through an alternate path without interrupting the ongoing session. This process is managed entirely by the protocol itself, transparent to the application, and executed without renegotiating the connection. The mechanism includes regular heartbeat messages and failover detection that monitor path availability and ensure that switching occurs quickly and without data loss. This type of resilience is critical in environments such as air traffic control or nuclear plant monitoring, where losing connection for even a few seconds is unacceptable.

Another vital aspect of SCTP that supports mission-critical operation is its chunk-based message delivery model. Unlike TCP, which delivers data as a continuous byte stream, SCTP transmits data in discrete messages, preserving message boundaries. This is particularly important in systems where command precision and message framing are integral to the operation. When messages must arrive intact and clearly delineated, as in control system commands or status notifications, SCTP ensures that the data arrives exactly as it was sent, eliminating the need for application-level message reconstruction. The reduction in protocol-induced ambiguity simplifies application design and decreases the risk of misinterpretation or command failure.

In mission-critical systems, message prioritization and delivery control are also essential. SCTP supports multistreaming, which allows multiple independent logical data streams within a single association. Each stream operates with its own sequence numbers and ordering guarantees. This feature prevents head-of-line blocking, a major issue in TCP where a delayed or lost packet blocks the delivery of all subsequent data. With SCTP, control messages, real-time updates, and routine logs can each be assigned to separate streams. Even if a less critical message is delayed or lost, the urgent ones continue to flow without interruption. This segmentation of data traffic ensures timely delivery of the most important information, aligning with the operational priorities of mission-critical applications.

Reliability in SCTP is further reinforced through its built-in support for selective acknowledgment and efficient retransmission strategies. SCTP receivers inform the sender of exactly which data chunks were received and which were not, allowing precise and minimal retransmissions. This selective retransmission reduces latency, conserves bandwidth, and ensures that recovery from packet loss does not lead to unnecessary data duplication. In critical infrastructure, where bandwidth may be limited or controlled by strict quality of service policies, this efficiency becomes a substantial advantage. It ensures that the network remains responsive and predictable, even in the presence of loss or delay.

Security is another key requirement in mission-critical systems, particularly in sectors that handle sensitive or classified data. SCTP includes authentication mechanisms that protect against spoofing and session hijacking. Through the use of cryptographic message authentication codes included in AUTH chunks, SCTP ensures that only authorized endpoints can send valid control or data chunks. The protocol's four-way handshake also protects against common denial-of-service attacks that exploit TCP's stateful connection setup. SCTP's stateless initiation mechanism means that servers do not commit resources until the client has proven its authenticity by returning a valid cookie, making it much harder for attackers to flood the system with fake connection attempts. In systems with national security or public safety implications, these protections are indispensable.

SCTP also allows for partial reliability, an optional extension useful in scenarios where real-time performance outweighs the need for guaranteed delivery. For example, in voice communications used by emergency services or drone telemetry where new position data constantly supersedes old, retransmitting lost packets may be counterproductive. SCTP allows the application to specify expiration policies for messages, after which the message is discarded if it has not yet been delivered. This capability ensures that system responsiveness is preserved without flooding the network with outdated information.

The ability to dynamically reconfigure associations is another powerful feature that supports mission-critical deployment. Using address configuration change chunks, endpoints can add or remove IP addresses during the lifetime of an association. This allows systems to adapt to changing network topologies, mobile environments, or hardware reassignments without breaking existing sessions. In defense applications or mobile medical units where nodes frequently join and leave different networks, this feature allows SCTP to maintain long-lived and adaptive associations that follow the operational context of the system rather than being tied to a static network configuration.

Real-time monitoring of SCTP behavior is possible through built-in diagnostic messages and system calls that expose internal association status, buffer sizes, and retransmission events. These diagnostics can be integrated into supervisory software or alerting systems, enabling operators to detect potential issues before they result in failure. Combined with external tools like Wireshark and performance monitoring dashboards, engineers can track every aspect of SCTP performance, from individual stream delays to congestion control behavior. This observability is essential for maintaining high confidence in system behavior and compliance with operational standards.

SCTP's capabilities are already being used in telecommunications core networks, industrial control systems, and military communication platforms, each of which exemplifies the demand for high resilience, deterministic performance, and security. Its standardized design, combined with support in major operating systems and mature APIs, allows it to be integrated into a wide variety of applications without reliance on proprietary solutions. As digital infrastructure continues to expand into domains where uptime and precision are paramount, SCTP's design principles offer a dependable transport layer that meets the demanding requirements of mission-critical environments.

Future Directions in SCTP Standardization

The Stream Control Transmission Protocol was designed to address the limitations of traditional transport protocols, introducing features like multistreaming, multihoming, message orientation, and improved security. Since its standardization in the early 2000s through RFC 2960 and its updates such as RFC 4960, SCTP has gained steady recognition in domains requiring high reliability and resilience. While SCTP has not achieved the ubiquity of TCP or UDP in everyday internet traffic, its adoption in telecom infrastructure, WebRTC, industrial control, and real-time systems has demonstrated its potential. As technology and network architectures continue to evolve, the future of SCTP standardization lies in adapting to modern requirements, resolving long-standing implementation challenges, and aligning with emerging paradigms such as QUIC, 5G, edge computing, and post-quantum cryptography. The future trajectory of SCTP standardization will be shaped by several core objectives: expanding use-case compatibility, simplifying deployment across modern stacks, improving security primitives, and integrating with next-generation protocols.

One of the most critical areas of future standardization involves enhancing SCTP's compatibility with NATs and firewalls. While SCTP was originally designed for trusted, managed environments like telecommunications networks, today's internet relies heavily on devices operating behind NATs, firewalls, and other middleboxes that expect TCP or UDP traffic. SCTP's use of a distinct IP protocol number (132) means it is often blocked or not fully understood by intermediary devices. The ongoing effort to standardize SCTP encapsulation over UDP, as described in drafts such as SCTP-over-UDP, is a step toward solving this issue. By encapsulating SCTP packets within UDP datagrams, implementations can traverse existing NAT infrastructure without modification, enabling deployment in broader consumer and enterprise contexts. Standardization of this method, including port conventions, encapsulation headers, and fallback mechanisms, is essential for consistent behavior across vendors and operating systems.

Another future direction is refining SCTP's support for modern application-layer protocols and paradigms. With the proliferation of real-time applications, IoT systems, and event-driven microservices, protocols are increasingly expected to support rich session semantics, zero-round-trip startup, and fine-grained message control. While SCTP's message-based delivery and multistreaming capabilities already align well with these needs, additional extensions are being considered to make it more suitable for dynamic and elastic workloads. This includes support for dynamic stream creation and reconfiguration, where associations could be modified on-the-fly to adjust to changes in application logic or connection requirements. Enhancing the scalability of stream identifiers and improving signaling for stream management will help SCTP accommodate a broader range of real-time applications without requiring connection renegotiation or application restarts.

Security is another focal point for future SCTP standardization. Although SCTP provides built-in mechanisms for verifying association integrity, such as cookies and verification tags, it does not offer end-to-end encryption or forward secrecy on its own. In secure environments, SCTP is often combined with IPsec or DTLS to protect data in transit.

However, these layers introduce complexity and dependency on external key management systems. Future enhancements could include tighter integration with emerging cryptographic frameworks, including support for hybrid post-quantum key exchange algorithms and simplified negotiation of security parameters. Additionally, standardizing SCTP profiles that mandate certain levels of authentication and encryption could help streamline adoption in regulated industries and environments with strict compliance requirements.

As networking continues to shift toward software-defined infrastructure and programmable control planes, SCTP's standardization may also explore how to better support software-defined networking (SDN) and network function virtualization (NFV). SCTP's path management and failover mechanisms are well-suited to dynamic network topologies, but standardized APIs for interaction with SDN controllers could allow SCTP endpoints to dynamically adjust path selection, stream priorities, or failover thresholds based on real-time network telemetry. This would allow SCTP to adapt more intelligently to traffic patterns, congestion, or link failure, improving performance and reducing downtime. Standardization efforts in this space could define control interfaces and behaviors that allow SCTP to be treated as a first-class citizen in programmable networks.

Interoperability remains a challenge in SCTP's evolution and an area that demands continued focus in standardization. Although the protocol is implemented in major operating systems and is used in specific applications like WebRTC and telecom signaling, variation in feature support and behavior between implementations has created fragmentation. Some stacks support only a subset of extensions such as PR-SCTP or authentication, and differences in API behavior, default parameters, and stream handling can lead to inconsistencies. Future standardization must focus on clearer compliance levels and certification processes that define mandatory features and testable behaviors. By improving conformance testing and reference implementations, SCTP can gain the predictability required for broader adoption.

In addition to extensions and implementation alignment, SCTP must evolve alongside other transport protocols. The emergence of QUIC, a transport protocol built on UDP and designed to replace TCP and TLS in many use cases, has prompted renewed interest in transport-layer innovation. QUIC incorporates many SCTP-like features, including stream multiplexing, congestion control, and message framing, but does so with a focus on encryption and performance. Rather than viewing QUIC and SCTP as competitors, future SCTP standardization may look at interoperability or hybrid approaches. For instance, there may be value in standardizing a mapping of SCTP semantics onto QUIC's transport primitives or creating SCTP-compatible modes within the QUIC ecosystem. Alternatively, SCTP could serve as a foundation for specialized applications where QUIC's encrypted-by-default model is not ideal, such as in regulated industrial environments or legacy telecom infrastructure.

There is also a strong case for updating SCTP's specifications to improve readability, modernize terminology, and reflect contemporary best practices in protocol design. RFC 4960, while comprehensive, was authored in an era before widespread use of JSON, RESTful services, containerized workloads, and zero-trust architectures. A new generation of developers and network engineers would benefit from refreshed documentation that includes deployment patterns, example configurations, and clearer guidance on how SCTP fits into modern architectures. Complementary efforts could include standardizing protocol diagnostics, telemetry formats, and integration with observability platforms that are now common in DevOps and Site Reliability Engineering workflows.

The future of SCTP standardization will depend not only on technical enhancements but also on community engagement and industry alignment. Encouraging contributions from cloud providers, equipment manufacturers, developers of real-time systems, and open-source projects is essential to building momentum. Promoting interoperability hackathons, maintaining updated conformance test suites, and aligning with broader IETF transport initiatives will position SCTP as a sustainable and evolving standard. As transport needs become more demanding and diverse, SCTP's flexibility and robustness remain highly relevant, and with continued standardization effort, the protocol is well-positioned to support the next generation of resilient, intelligent, and secure networked applications.

Challenges in SCTP Deployment

Deploying the Stream Control Transmission Protocol in modern networks presents a unique set of challenges that extend beyond protocol design and into the realms of infrastructure compatibility, developer adoption, application support, and network policy enforcement. While SCTP offers compelling advantages over traditional transport protocols like TCP and UDP—including multistreaming, multihoming, message orientation, and built-in support for partial reliability—its broader deployment has been hindered by numerous technical and operational hurdles. These challenges must be addressed systematically to unlock the full potential of SCTP in production environments across industries.

One of the most immediate and persistent challenges is the lack of universal support for SCTP in middleboxes such as routers, firewalls, and Network Address Translation devices. SCTP uses its own IP protocol number, 132, and many network devices are either unaware of this protocol or explicitly block non-TCP/UDP traffic for security and simplicity reasons. As a result, SCTP traffic is frequently dropped at the perimeter of enterprise and service provider networks. While encapsulation methods such as SCTP-over-UDP have been proposed and partially implemented to enable SCTP to traverse these network devices, standardization is still in progress, and not all operating systems or libraries support this feature natively. Without reliable traversal mechanisms, deploying SCTP across the public internet or in multi-tenant environments remains problematic.

Another deployment challenge lies in limited support across programming languages and application frameworks. While the SCTP socket API is defined and implemented in operating systems like Linux, FreeBSD, and Windows, high-level languages such as JavaScript, Python, and even some versions of Java do not expose native bindings for SCTP. This forces developers to rely on C extensions or external libraries, increasing complexity and limiting portability. As modern application development increasingly relies on cross-platform tools, microservices, and containerized environments, the absence of seamless SCTP support in mainstream frameworks discourages developers from adopting it as a default transport layer. Efforts to integrate SCTP into popular frameworks must be strengthened to reduce the learning curve and friction for new adopters.

Integration with cloud infrastructure presents additional obstacles. Public cloud providers like AWS, Azure, and Google Cloud Platform primarily design their networks around TCP and UDP, with specific firewall rules, security groups, and load balancing services optimized for those protocols. SCTP is generally not treated as a first-class citizen in these environments, leading to unpredictable behavior or outright incompatibility. For instance, SCTP traffic may not be allowed through virtual private cloud boundaries or may be unsupported by managed load balancers. Cloud-native deployments that require SCTP must often resort to complex workarounds, including tunneling through VPNs, setting up custom routing rules, or hosting SCTP-enabled workloads on bare-metal instances. These workarounds undermine the simplicity and agility that cloud computing promises, making SCTP less appealing for DevOps teams and platform architects.

Operational visibility and monitoring also pose a challenge. Popular observability tools used in cloud-native environments—such as Prometheus, Grafana, and OpenTelemetry—are deeply integrated with TCP and HTTP metrics but lack built-in support for SCTP-specific events. Metrics like per-stream latency, chunk retransmission counts, and path failover events are critical to understanding SCTP performance but are not exposed in conventional logging or telemetry pipelines. Without native support in monitoring stacks, network engineers and SREs must develop custom exporters or rely on packet capture tools like Wireshark, which are not easily integrated into real-time operational dashboards. This limits the ability to detect issues, tune performance, or conduct effective postmortem analysis.

Security policies in many enterprises present another significant hurdle. Because SCTP is less familiar to many IT administrators and security professionals, it is often excluded from baseline configurations and threat models. Firewalls may be configured to reject SCTP traffic by default, and intrusion detection systems may not have adequate signatures or behavioral models to inspect SCTP flows. This leads to a perception that SCTP introduces additional risk or administrative overhead. Educating security teams about SCTP's authentication features, stateful handshake, and resistance to common attacks is necessary to increase confidence in its deployment. Standardizing secure-by-default SCTP profiles, especially for public-facing services, could help address this concern.

Cross-platform interoperability is another barrier to SCTP deployment. Even though the protocol has been standardized and implemented in various operating systems, differences in interpretation of optional features, default parameter values, and socket behavior can lead to incompatibility between peers. For example, support for partial reliability, authentication chunks, or dynamic address reconfiguration may vary across platforms. These inconsistencies lead to subtle bugs and make it difficult to achieve predictable behavior in heterogeneous environments. Comprehensive conformance testing, cross-vendor certification, and clearer documentation of mandatory versus optional features are essential to mitigate these issues and foster trust in SCTP implementations.

From a performance standpoint, SCTP can also be more resource-intensive than simpler transport protocols. The additional logic required for stream management, chunk handling, and multihoming increases CPU and memory usage, especially in high-throughput or low-latency applications. When deploying SCTP in environments with limited processing power or strict energy budgets—such as IoT gateways or embedded systems—these resource costs can become prohibitive. While SCTP's advanced features often justify the overhead, performance tuning and lightweight profiles may be required to make it viable in constrained environments. These optimizations must be documented and standardized to ensure predictable resource consumption.

The perception of SCTP as a niche protocol further complicates deployment. Despite its technical merits, SCTP is still largely associated with telecom signaling, rather than being viewed as a general-purpose transport option. This limits its adoption in web-scale systems and enterprise applications. Changing this perception requires more success stories, community engagement, and broader inclusion in open-source projects. SCTP must be positioned not just as a specialized solution but as a versatile alternative capable of improving performance, reliability, and security in a wide array of scenarios.

Efforts to deploy SCTP must also address the gap between research and practice. Many academic papers and experimental implementations demonstrate SCTP's strengths, but these findings are not always translated into production-grade tools or commercial software. Bridging this gap requires collaboration between academia, industry, and standards bodies to ensure that innovations in SCTP protocol behavior, congestion control, or failover logic are reflected in mature and well-maintained codebases. Long-term support, community maintenance, and funding for open-source SCTP stacks are crucial to this effort.

Overcoming these deployment challenges is critical to realizing the benefits of SCTP in modern, real-time, and distributed systems. By addressing infrastructure compatibility, improving developer experience, enhancing visibility and security, and fostering cross-platform consistency, SCTP can fulfill its promise as a transport protocol designed for the next generation of networked applications.

Application-Layer Protocol Integration

Integrating the Stream Control Transmission Protocol with application-layer protocols requires a strategic and carefully considered approach that accounts for SCTP's advanced capabilities and the diverse requirements of applications. Unlike TCP and UDP, which have long-standing conventions and widespread support in application protocol design, SCTP offers features like multistreaming, multihoming, message orientation, and partial reliability that significantly impact how data is organized, transmitted, and processed. Application developers who aim to leverage SCTP effectively must understand how to align their protocol semantics with SCTP's transport characteristics while accommodating deployment constraints and interoperability considerations.

One of the first principles in integrating SCTP with application-layer protocols is understanding its message-oriented nature. While TCP presents a continuous byte stream to the application, requiring additional framing mechanisms to delineate logical messages, SCTP maintains message boundaries natively. This property simplifies protocol design, as developers can treat each application-level message as a self-contained unit without worrying about stream reassembly or delimiter scanning. However, developers must also consider message size limitations imposed by the path Maximum Transmission Unit, since large messages may be fragmented into multiple chunks during transmission. SCTP handles reassembly, but applications should still be designed to produce efficiently sized messages to minimize delay and memory usage.

Multistreaming allows applications to define multiple logical channels within a single SCTP association, with each stream operating independently in terms of ordering. Application-layer protocols that involve concurrent activities, such as control signaling, telemetry reporting, or media transport, can assign each activity to a separate stream. This design prevents head-of-line blocking and improves responsiveness, as delays or losses in one stream do not affect others. When integrating with SCTP, developers should identify natural divisions within their protocol flows that benefit from such separation. For example, in a chat application, control messages such as presence updates and typing indicators can be sent over separate streams from the actual chat messages. Similarly, in a remote instrumentation protocol, command requests and continuous data reports can be kept on different streams for better prioritization and reliability control.

Partial reliability is another critical feature that enhances SCTP's suitability for modern application protocols. In many real-time or time-sensitive contexts, not all data requires guaranteed delivery. SCTP allows applications to specify expiration parameters for each message, such as a maximum retransmission count or time-to-live, after which the message is discarded if not yet acknowledged. This aligns well with use cases like live video, sensor updates, or trading data where old messages lose value quickly. Application designers must map their data categories to appropriate reliability models, deciding which messages can be sent with partial reliability and which require full retransmission guarantees. The resulting application-layer protocol becomes more efficient and responsive, particularly under constrained network conditions.

Integrating SCTP with existing application-layer protocols often involves adapting legacy designs built on TCP or UDP. Many established protocols assume TCP's ordered byte stream or UDP's unordered datagram semantics, which differ significantly from SCTP's hybrid model. When retrofitting such protocols to work over SCTP, developers must revisit assumptions about framing, sequencing, and delivery behavior. Protocols that rely on strict ordering may need to be constrained to a single SCTP stream or implement additional ordering logic. Conversely, those that can benefit from SCTP's multistreaming must be redesigned to explicitly assign messages to streams and manage their lifecycles independently. This process often reveals inefficiencies or design limitations in the original protocol and provides opportunities for optimization.

Security integration at the application layer must also account for SCTP's features. Although SCTP includes basic authentication and integrity checking mechanisms, application-layer protocols frequently require end-to-end encryption and detailed identity verification. Integrating SCTP with Transport Layer Security or Datagram TLS involves careful coordination of handshake timing, key management, and session resumption strategies. The encapsulation of SCTP over DTLS is especially relevant in WebRTC applications, where SCTP is used for the data channel and must coexist with media streams secured by SRTP. Application protocols built on SCTP should include clear guidelines for initializing secure associations, negotiating features, and verifying peer capabilities without exposing vulnerabilities or leaking sensitive data during the handshake process.

Compatibility with multiplexed environments is another factor that influences integration. In microservice-based architectures or multiplexed transport layers like QUIC, application-layer protocols may need to share connections or work within a virtualized transport context. SCTP's inherent support for multiplexing via multistreaming provides a natural fit, but the protocol must be integrated with stream identification and control mechanisms at the application level. Stream identifiers must be mapped to logical sessions or transactions, and applications must handle stream closure, resets, and retries in a way that preserves consistency. This is particularly important in protocols that support simultaneous user sessions or parallel task execution, where isolation and ordering constraints vary across use cases.

To facilitate broad adoption and ease integration, libraries and frameworks that abstract SCTP behavior are essential. These middleware components should expose a clean API that allows applications to send and receive messages without managing low-level socket details. They should also provide hooks for reliability settings, stream management, and security configuration. Developers can then focus on protocol logic and data structures rather than transport mechanics. Language bindings in Python, Java, Go, and Rust would significantly accelerate the adoption of SCTP by application developers who lack the time or expertise to work directly with raw sockets.

Application-layer debugging tools must evolve alongside SCTP integration. Existing tools like Wireshark already provide excellent visibility into SCTP streams and chunks, but higher-level logging and diagnostics at the application protocol layer can further simplify troubleshooting. Tracing tools should log message delivery status, stream assignments, and retransmission behavior in a format accessible to developers and operations teams. Monitoring stream health, delivery latency, and message drop rates helps identify bottlenecks and optimize protocol performance under real-world conditions.

Finally, integrating SCTP with application-layer protocols benefits from community engagement and shared best practices. Documentation, examples, and open-source reference implementations can demonstrate how to use SCTP effectively in diverse scenarios. Protocol specifications should include profiles for SCTP usage, describing expected stream behavior, reliability settings, and fallback options. Collaboration between protocol designers and transport experts can yield robust, scalable, and secure applications that leverage the full potential of SCTP.

By aligning application-layer protocol design with SCTP's strengths, developers can achieve greater efficiency, flexibility, and robustness. Whether building real-time systems, collaborative applications, or industrial control interfaces, SCTP provides a transport foundation that adapts to modern needs while offering powerful tools for precision and performance. Thoughtful integration ensures that the advantages of SCTP are realized across the stack, delivering value in systems where traditional protocols fall short.

SCTP in Edge and Fog Computing

As modern computing architectures increasingly shift toward decentralized models such as edge and fog computing, the transport protocols that underpin communication in these systems must evolve to meet the demands of low latency, high reliability, dynamic topologies, and robust failure recovery. The Stream Control Transmission Protocol, originally developed for reliable signaling in telecommunication networks, is uniquely positioned to serve as a foundation for these next-generation computing paradigms. With features like multihoming, multistreaming, message orientation, and built-in support for failover, SCTP offers inherent advantages for edge and fog environments that must operate under varying network conditions, across heterogeneous devices, and within mission-critical applications.

Edge computing pushes processing and data storage closer to the source of data generation, typically at or near the endpoints, such as sensors, cameras, vehicles, and industrial machines. Fog computing complements this by providing an intermediate layer between the edge and the cloud, enabling distributed processing, storage, and control across network nodes. These architectures reduce the burden on centralized data centers, improve responsiveness, and support real-time analytics. However, they also introduce challenges related to dynamic network behavior, fluctuating connectivity, mobility, and the need for fast failover mechanisms. SCTP addresses many of these concerns directly through its transport-level capabilities.

One of the most relevant features of SCTP in the edge and fog context is its support for multihoming. Devices and nodes in a fog architecture may have multiple network interfaces, including Ethernet, Wi-Fi, cellular, or even satellite connections. SCTP allows a single association to span multiple IP addresses, enabling it to continue functioning even if one path becomes unavailable. This is especially critical in mobile and semi-mobile edge deployments, such as connected vehicles, drones, or remote monitoring stations. When a primary path fails, SCTP can seamlessly switch to an alternate address without requiring a session teardown or application intervention. This ensures continuous data flow and minimizes service disruption, which is vital for time-sensitive operations like remote diagnostics, predictive maintenance, and autonomous control.

Multistreaming, another core feature of SCTP, allows concurrent data flows within a single connection without interference. In edge and fog deployments, devices often need to transmit diverse types of data simultaneously, such as control commands, sensor data, firmware updates, and logs. SCTP enables each of these data types to be assigned to an independent stream, preserving ordering where needed and avoiding head-of-line blocking across unrelated messages. This optimizes performance and ensures that critical messages, such as emergency shutdown commands or safety alerts, are not delayed by bulk data transmissions. In industrial automation or healthcare applications running on fog architectures, such determinism and stream separation significantly enhance safety and operational efficiency.

SCTP's message-oriented nature provides further advantages for edge and fog systems. In contrast to TCP's byte-stream model, SCTP preserves application-level message boundaries, allowing each message to be interpreted directly without additional framing logic. This reduces parsing overhead, simplifies protocol implementation, and eliminates ambiguity during data interpretation. Edge nodes that process incoming data in real time benefit from this clarity, as it facilitates immediate decision-making and faster execution. Whether dealing with environmental sensors reporting temperature spikes or security cameras detecting motion anomalies, the ability to receive self-contained messages without reconstruction delays is crucial for timely action.

The partial reliability extension of SCTP is particularly well-suited for use cases at the edge where not all data has equal value over time. For instance, periodic telemetry from sensors may lose relevance quickly, and retransmitting outdated values can waste bandwidth and processing power. SCTP allows messages to be marked with expiration conditions, such as delivery deadlines or retry limits. If the conditions are not met, the message is discarded rather than retransmitted. This behavior aligns perfectly with edge analytics, where recent data is often more valuable than complete data. Applications can prioritize freshness over completeness, ensuring that system behavior reflects the current state of the environment rather than outdated conditions.

Fog nodes often serve as aggregation and coordination points between multiple edge devices and the cloud. SCTP's efficient connection management, with its support for long-lived associations and dynamic address reconfiguration, allows fog nodes to maintain stable communication channels with both upward and downward nodes. When edge devices come online, migrate, or change IP addresses due to DHCP or mobile transitions, SCTP can adapt without restarting the connection. This continuity supports seamless service delivery, especially in use cases where persistent sessions are essential, such as voice communications, telemedicine, or collaborative robotics.

Security is another area where SCTP brings advantages to edge and fog deployments. The protocol's four-way handshake, which uses a cookie mechanism for validation, helps protect against resource exhaustion attacks, making it more resilient in exposed environments where devices might be accessible over the internet or from untrusted networks. SCTP also supports message authentication via HMAC, enabling endpoints to verify data integrity and source authenticity. This is vital in distributed architectures where central control may not always be available to intervene in case of anomalies. Secure transport at the protocol level complements application-layer encryption and supports zero-trust models increasingly adopted in edge security frameworks.

As edge computing increasingly integrates with cloud-native technologies such as containers and orchestration platforms, SCTP must coexist with modern deployment environments. Support for SCTP in container networking, service meshes, and virtual network functions is still developing, but the protocol's stateless association initiation and support for encapsulation over UDP make it compatible with the needs of microservices and elastic architectures. When used over UDP, SCTP gains the ability to traverse NATs and firewalls more effectively, extending its reach to constrained edge devices and home or office deployments behind complex network topologies.

Operational visibility and observability are critical in distributed fog networks, where failures must be detected and resolved quickly. SCTP provides detailed feedback through heartbeat messages, chunk acknowledgment, and retransmission tracking, which can be captured by monitoring systems to evaluate link health, message loss, and latency trends. Edge and fog nodes equipped with such insights can make intelligent decisions about rerouting, service degradation, or node handover, contributing to self-healing and autonomic network behavior.

SCTP's deployment in edge and fog computing requires not only technical integration but also greater awareness and tooling support. Development environments must offer native bindings, protocol libraries, and diagnostics that make it easy for engineers to adopt SCTP in new applications. Training, reference implementations, and deployment guides will also play a role in demystifying SCTP's capabilities and encouraging its use in next-generation computing platforms.

As edge and fog computing continue to redefine the landscape of distributed processing and real-time interaction, the role of SCTP becomes increasingly important. Its design addresses many of the transport challenges inherent to decentralized, mobile, and resilient systems. By delivering reliable, efficient, and adaptable communication across dynamic topologies, SCTP provides a solid foundation for edge and fog architectures that must operate at the intersection of performance, security, and flexibility. Its integration into this space enables a new class of responsive, context-aware, and intelligent applications that extend the cloud's capabilities to the very edge of the network.

Case Studies in SCTP Deployment

The practical value of the Stream Control Transmission Protocol becomes most evident when examined through real-world deployments where its unique features have addressed critical challenges in communication, reliability, and system resilience. Across a range of industries, from telecommunications to industrial automation, SCTP has demonstrated its capacity to support demanding applications through multihoming, multistreaming, and its structured, message-oriented architecture. These case studies highlight how SCTP has been implemented in different domains, revealing not only the strengths of the protocol but also the strategies employed to overcome deployment barriers, integrate with legacy infrastructure, and meet strict operational requirements.

In the telecommunications industry, SCTP has been foundational in transporting signaling messages within core network components. The most widely known and enduring example is its role in the transport layer for the Signaling System 7 replacement protocol known as SS7 over IP, particularly through the use of the SIGTRAN suite. Protocols such as M3UA and SUA rely on SCTP to deliver signaling traffic between signaling gateways and media gateways. In this context, SCTP replaced TCP as the transport protocol due to its multihoming and multistreaming features, which are essential for maintaining carrier-grade uptime and performance. In a typical deployment by a European mobile network operator, SCTP was used to connect geographically redundant signaling servers over dual redundant fiber connections. Each server was configured with multiple IP addresses corresponding to separate network interfaces. When one path experienced a failure due to a fiber cut, SCTP automatically redirected traffic through the backup path without dropping the signaling association. This failover occurred within seconds and was entirely transparent to the higher-layer applications, which continued to process call signaling and mobility events without interruption.

In another scenario within the same telecom infrastructure, SCTP's multistreaming capability prevented head-of-line blocking during high volumes of simultaneous signaling messages. Each signaling context, such as call setup or SMS delivery, was mapped to a unique stream within the SCTP association. This prevented delayed or retransmitted messages from affecting unrelated transactions, a common issue when using TCP. As a result, the network operator reported increased signaling throughput and a reduction in latency-related anomalies during peak traffic periods.

Beyond telecommunications, SCTP has been successfully deployed in industrial automation environments, where real-time control and monitoring are crucial. In one example, a North American manufacturing company implemented SCTP as the transport layer for a factory-wide supervisory control and data acquisition system. The system included programmable logic controllers, human-machine interfaces, and a centralized control server that had to operate continuously across shifts and endure harsh environmental conditions. Each component in the system had multiple network interfaces for redundancy, and SCTP was configured to take advantage of multihoming to ensure uninterrupted communication even during switchovers or physical link failures. In addition to failover, SCTP's ability to deliver messages with preserved boundaries allowed for cleaner parsing of telemetry data, which was structured in discrete sensor reports and control commands. The engineering team reported that the switch to SCTP reduced the complexity of the control logic by removing the need for application-layer message reassembly, which had previously been required with TCP.

The banking and finance sector, known for its strict requirements around reliability, security, and performance, has also seen experimental and production deployments of SCTP in systems that support trading operations. In one case study, a financial services firm used SCTP in a data distribution platform responsible for real-time market data dissemination. The platform serviced dozens of downstream clients, each of which required near-instantaneous updates on market fluctuations. SCTP was selected due to its ability to maintain persistent associations across network transitions. The firm operated a network of trading gateways with primary and secondary uplinks to multiple data centers. SCTP ensured that in the event of a network fault or data center failover, the connections to client terminals were preserved and the stream of market data remained intact. Moreover, SCTP's partial reliability extension was used to prevent retransmission of stale market data updates, thereby conserving bandwidth and maintaining a more relevant view of the market for the trading algorithms. This implementation improved the responsiveness of the firm's trading systems while ensuring operational continuity during infrastructure maintenance or unexpected outages.

In the realm of academic and research networks, SCTP has also been utilized to support advanced communication between high-performance computing clusters. In a university research consortium that operated a grid computing network, SCTP was used to maintain persistent sessions between compute nodes across multiple campuses.

The multistreaming capability allowed control messages, job scheduling commands, and dataset transfers to be sent in parallel without mutual interference. Researchers observed fewer interruptions and reduced job completion times when SCTP was used in place of traditional TCP-based tools, especially during concurrent multi-node job execution. SCTP's support for dynamic address reconfiguration further enabled mobile nodes or dynamically assigned virtual machines to rejoin the network seamlessly, reducing the administrative burden of session reinitialization.

One final case study involves the use of SCTP in a national emergency communication system, where government and emergency services relied on resilient transport for the coordination of field operations. In this deployment, SCTP was embedded in mobile communication terminals carried by first responders and linked to command-and-control centers via cellular and satellite networks. The unpredictable nature of network availability in disaster zones made SCTP's failover capabilities invaluable. Mobile devices registered with multiple IP endpoints, and SCTP dynamically chose the best available path for each association. As emergency vehicles moved between coverage zones, SCTP transitioned connections across interfaces without the need for human intervention or loss of situational awareness. The system also utilized SCTP's heartbeat messages to continuously assess connection quality and preemptively reroute traffic when degradation was detected. The feedback provided by SCTP's built-in acknowledgment and retransmission features gave operations personnel visibility into the health of the communication network, enabling them to allocate resources more effectively.

Each of these case studies underscores SCTP's flexibility and robustness across a diverse set of domains. From telecom core networks to industrial systems, financial markets, research environments, and emergency response, SCTP has proven to be a transport protocol capable of meeting modern challenges with precision and resilience. The adoption of SCTP in these varied applications demonstrates that, while it may not be as universally deployed as TCP or UDP, it offers specific advantages that make it a superior choice for systems that cannot afford to compromise on reliability, timing, or fault tolerance. These real-world implementations continue to inform the evolution of SCTP and serve as blueprints for its use in the next generation of connected systems.

Performance Metrics and Evaluation

Evaluating the performance of the Stream Control Transmission Protocol requires a comprehensive understanding of both traditional transport metrics and the unique aspects of SCTP's architecture. Unlike TCP and UDP, SCTP introduces transport-layer features such as multistreaming, multihoming, message framing, and optional partial reliability. These features influence how performance is measured and what parameters are most critical to monitor in various applications. Whether SCTP is deployed in telecom signaling networks, real-time control systems, multimedia applications, or cloud-based services, the effectiveness of its deployment is determined by how well it meets specific performance goals related to throughput, latency, reliability, resilience, and resource efficiency.

Throughput is one of the most fundamental metrics in any transport protocol evaluation. In SCTP, throughput is influenced not only by congestion control and flow control mechanisms but also by the behavior of individual streams within an association. SCTP's congestion control operates similarly to TCP's, adjusting the congestion window based on acknowledgments and perceived loss. However, SCTP must manage congestion across all streams in a single association, and its chunk-based message handling can lead to different throughput characteristics depending on message sizes and stream multiplexing strategies. Tests comparing SCTP to TCP in bulk data transfers over stable links often show similar throughput under ideal conditions. However, in more complex topologies involving multistreaming or concurrent data types, SCTP can outperform TCP by avoiding head-of-line blocking and by delivering messages independently across streams.

Latency is another critical performance indicator, especially in applications requiring near real-time responsiveness. SCTP's latency behavior is shaped by several factors, including retransmission timeouts, chunk assembly, stream prioritization, and path selection.

Because SCTP supports unordered delivery and partial reliability, applications can configure associations to minimize latency by discarding stale messages or avoiding retransmission delays for non-critical data. The protocol also supports path probing and failover through heartbeat mechanisms, which introduce minimal overhead but must be tuned to avoid unnecessary latency during failover detection. Evaluations of SCTP in low-latency environments, such as online gaming or financial data distribution, often highlight its ability to maintain consistent delivery timing even when one network path becomes congested or unreliable.

Reliability in SCTP is not absolute by default but is configurable. Evaluating reliability involves measuring packet loss rates, retransmission efficiency, and recovery times under varying conditions. SCTP's selective acknowledgment mechanism enables fine-grained recovery by indicating exactly which chunks have been received, thus allowing retransmission of only the missing pieces. This selective retransmission reduces the burden on the network and speeds up recovery compared to full retransmission approaches. In systems where reliability is mission critical, such as SCADA or telecommunications signaling, SCTP's chunk delivery guarantees have been shown to provide higher assurance levels than those achievable with UDP and less overhead than TCP in environments with frequent message loss.

Resilience is a performance domain where SCTP significantly differentiates itself. The ability to maintain communication sessions across multiple IP paths without interruption is central to SCTP's design. Performance evaluations in this area focus on failover time, packet loss during path transitions, and session continuity. In controlled experiments simulating link failure, SCTP consistently demonstrates sub-second failover times when heartbeat intervals and thresholds are properly configured. These measurements are critical in assessing SCTP's value in mobile, wireless, or multi-homed environments, where constant connectivity is not guaranteed. Path management metrics such as primary path switching latency, retransmission behavior during recovery, and heartbeat failure detection time provide a detailed picture of SCTP's resilience performance.

Efficiency, both in terms of bandwidth utilization and resource consumption, is a practical aspect of SCTP performance evaluation. Because SCTP includes additional headers for chunk structure and optional parameters, its per-packet overhead is slightly greater than that of TCP or UDP. However, this is often offset by reduced need for application-layer framing, fewer retransmissions, and the ability to carry multiple logical streams in one association. Evaluating efficiency requires profiling CPU and memory usage under high-load conditions, especially when managing many concurrent streams or associations. Measurements in cloud-based systems and data centers often show that SCTP performs well under parallel workloads and can support a high number of active streams without linear increases in overhead, thanks to its internal stream sequencing and association management design.

In testing environments, benchmarking SCTP performance also involves assessing startup time and association setup behavior. The four-way handshake used in SCTP introduces a small delay compared to TCP's three-way handshake but enhances security and mitigates denial-of-service risk. Performance testing during burst traffic or high connection churn can reveal how quickly SCTP servers respond to new association requests and how efficiently resources are allocated. Connection establishment time, initial congestion window performance, and stream availability on startup are all metrics that contribute to evaluating SCTP's responsiveness in elastic service environments.

Jitter, or variation in packet arrival time, is another metric that affects perceived performance in streaming and voice applications. SCTP's ability to assign different reliability and ordering requirements to each stream can help minimize jitter for time-sensitive data while buffering or reordering other types of messages. Performance evaluations in media streaming scenarios often measure frame arrival intervals, out-of-order delivery rate, and mean opinion scores (MOS) to determine user-perceived quality. SCTP's stream separation can reduce jitter introduced by buffering and allow smoother playback, particularly in video conferencing or real-time collaboration tools.

Security-related performance metrics also matter in SCTP evaluations. When authentication chunks are used or when SCTP is deployed over

DTLS or IPsec, the computational cost of cryptographic operations must be measured alongside traditional transport performance. Encryption latency, handshake processing time, and key exchange duration become part of the overall performance profile. These metrics are especially important in edge devices, embedded systems, or mobile platforms where compute resources are limited. Evaluating SCTP with security overhead reveals trade-offs that may influence configuration decisions in secure deployments.

Scalability is a final dimension of performance evaluation for SCTP. Large-scale deployments, such as those in telecom signaling backbones or cloud-based APIs, require SCTP to manage thousands of concurrent associations, often with diverse stream and path configurations. Testing under simulated scale involves measuring throughput, latency, and memory footprint as the number of active associations increases. It also includes examining control-plane behavior such as heartbeat management, association teardown, and stream reconfiguration. These measurements help determine the suitability of SCTP in scenarios involving massive IoT networks, real-time analytics pipelines, or federated systems spanning multiple locations.

By measuring performance across all these dimensions—throughput, latency, reliability, resilience, efficiency, scalability, and security— engineers and researchers can gain a complete understanding of SCTP's capabilities and limitations. This enables informed deployment decisions, optimal tuning, and the development of robust applications that take full advantage of SCTP's sophisticated transport architecture. Careful performance evaluation also ensures that SCTP implementations meet the expectations of diverse use cases, from high-speed financial data feeds to resilient industrial control systems and beyond.

Designing Robust Applications with SCTP

Designing robust applications with the Stream Control Transmission Protocol involves leveraging its advanced transport features to build systems that are resilient to failure, efficient in performance, and adaptable to changing network conditions. Robustness in application design is not only about avoiding crashes or errors but also about ensuring that the application continues to operate correctly and efficiently even under stress, network instability, partial outages, or unexpected traffic conditions. SCTP was designed with this robustness in mind, offering developers a transport layer that surpasses TCP and UDP in flexibility, reliability, and control. Applications that integrate SCTP effectively can take advantage of features such as multistreaming, multihoming, partial reliability, and strong message integrity to deliver services that maintain quality and consistency in the face of real-world challenges.

A key principle in designing robust applications with SCTP is understanding and properly utilizing its multistreaming capability. Multistreaming allows an application to create multiple logical streams within a single SCTP association, each with its own sequence numbering and delivery ordering. This enables developers to separate different classes of data so that a delay or retransmission in one stream does not block the others. For instance, in a video surveillance system, control commands, metadata, and video frames can be assigned to separate streams. Even if a video frame is lost and needs to be retransmitted, control commands for adjusting the camera angle or updating system parameters can continue without delay. This separation enhances responsiveness and maintains operational consistency, especially in environments where data prioritization and flow isolation are critical.

Multihoming is another cornerstone feature that contributes to robust application design. It allows each endpoint in an SCTP association to advertise multiple IP addresses, enabling communication to continue seamlessly if one network path fails. Applications that are deployed in mobile environments, remote locations, or redundant data centers can benefit from SCTP's ability to reroute traffic without dropping the session. For developers, this means designing applications that can detect and respond to path changes without requiring a full reconnection. Health checks, retries, and failover logic that might be necessary when using TCP can be handled by SCTP internally. Applications can simply remain operational and allow the protocol to ensure continuity. When combined with external monitoring, the application can report status or adjust behavior based on real-time information about the path currently in use, improving observability and fault diagnosis.

Another critical aspect of designing robust applications with SCTP is taking advantage of its message-oriented nature. Unlike TCP, which treats data as a continuous stream of bytes, SCTP maintains the boundaries of each message. This simplifies the parsing process and avoids the need for application-layer framing, which can often introduce bugs or lead to misinterpretation of message contents. In systems where message integrity and structure are essential, such as financial trading platforms or control systems in automation, being able to send and receive complete messages with guaranteed boundaries reduces the likelihood of data corruption and improves the reliability of data processing pipelines.

Applications can further enhance robustness by using SCTP's partial reliability extension to differentiate between critical and non-critical data. In many real-world systems, not all data must be delivered reliably. Sensor readings, telemetry data, or time-sensitive alerts may become irrelevant if delayed. By assigning expiration times or retry limits to such messages, applications can ensure that stale data is not retransmitted unnecessarily, thereby saving bandwidth and reducing congestion. This allows the application to focus on the most relevant and timely data, improving overall performance and user experience. For example, in a drone fleet management system, current GPS coordinates may only be useful within a specific time window. If a packet containing coordinates is delayed beyond that window, retransmitting it provides no benefit. SCTP allows the developer to configure the protocol to drop the expired message and proceed with newer data, ensuring that decisions are always based on the most accurate information available.

Security also plays a fundamental role in application robustness, and SCTP includes mechanisms to prevent common threats that compromise stability and integrity. The four-way handshake process using cookies protects servers from SYN flooding attacks by ensuring that resources are only committed after verifying the legitimacy of the client. SCTP also supports authentication chunks for validating the integrity and authenticity of messages. Applications that rely on sensitive data transfers or control instructions can enable these features to prevent tampering and unauthorized access. For applications in healthcare, public safety, or industrial control, where malicious interference can have serious consequences, incorporating SCTP's built-in security features into the overall security model contributes directly to system robustness.

To fully exploit SCTP's capabilities, developers should also focus on designing applications that adapt dynamically to network conditions. This includes monitoring round-trip times, retransmission statistics, and stream-level delivery metrics provided by SCTP. With this information, applications can adjust their behavior, such as modifying message frequency, changing the priority of certain streams, or temporarily disabling less important data flows during congestion. Adaptive behavior ensures that applications remain functional and efficient even when network performance degrades.

The robustness of SCTP-based applications also depends on proper handling of association lifecycle events. Applications must be prepared for association startup delays, path verification processes, and graceful shutdowns. Clean termination and state management prevent resource leaks and ensure that reconnection attempts are well-timed and controlled. SCTP provides specific events for association state changes, which developers can handle through event-driven logic to maintain system integrity and improve fault tolerance. For example, an application might pause data processing during an association reconfiguration or failover and resume once confirmation of a stable path is received.

Logging and diagnostics are important tools in building robust applications. Because SCTP exposes detailed state and behavior information, including acknowledgment status, stream identifiers, chunk types, and retransmission events, developers can instrument their applications with fine-grained logs that support troubleshooting and performance tuning. This visibility allows for proactive maintenance and faster recovery from unexpected issues. Additionally, integrating these metrics with monitoring systems ensures that performance anomalies or protocol-level errors are detected early and acted upon before they impact users or downstream systems.

Robust application design also benefits from modular, reusable components that abstract SCTP's complexity while exposing its flexibility. Encapsulating SCTP interaction within middleware or communication libraries allows developers to focus on application logic while relying on well-tested modules to manage streams, handle partial reliability settings, and perform path management. This modular approach improves maintainability and reduces the risk of introducing bugs during updates or scaling efforts.

By taking full advantage of SCTP's design and aligning application architecture with its transport semantics, developers can create systems that are not only resilient but also capable of maintaining high performance and functional accuracy under a wide range of operating conditions. This robustness becomes a defining characteristic of the application, setting it apart in terms of reliability, user experience, and operational longevity. In an increasingly connected and data-driven world, building applications on top of a transport protocol like SCTP empowers developers to meet the growing expectations of responsiveness, fault tolerance, and adaptability.

www.ingramcontent.com/pod-product-compliance
Lightning Source LLC
La Vergne TN
LVHW051238050326
832903LV00028B/2459